COO

Game Birds

Scott & Tiffany Haugen

H E

DEDICATION

*T*his book is dedicated to all the wingshooters who can't wait to get in the field and gather delectable upland birds and waterfowl all season long. It's also for those hunters who live for the hunt yet are apprehensive when preparing their quarry.

We all share the same passion, and it's our fondest hope you'll benefit from the years of work, experimentation and resourcefulness that went in to the creation of this book.

Happy hunting and God bless!

Published in 2011 by HAUGEN ENTERPRISES

Photography: Scott and Tiffany Haugen

Spiral bound ISBN-13: 978-0-9819423-3-9
Spiral bound UPC: 0-81127-00327-3
Printed in China

Contents

ACKNOWLEDGEMENTS

*T*hanks to all those people who helped out over the years it took to develop and create this book. To you taste-testers and cooks who were willing to try things with an open mind, thank you.

A special thanks goes out to our sons, who not only helped us gather birds for this book, but assisted in the cleaning, preparation and recipe development.

We couldn't have done it without you!

Tiffany and Braxton.

Kazden and Scott.

INTRODUCTION

*G*rowing up in Oregon's game-rich Willamette Valley, we were both fortunate to have game birds as part of many meals. But it wasn't until we were married that we made the conscious choice to make game birds a staple in our diets. Most of the first decade of our marriage found us living a subsistence lifestyle in the Alaskan bush, where we were school teachers.

Leaving the world of teaching behind, the next 10 years found us embarking on new careers back in the land where we were raised. Although we went from ptarmigan and sea ducks back to turkey, grouse, quail and geese, many of the preparation and cooking methods remained the same. In the past 20 years, we have roasted, baked, fried, sauteed, grilled, slow cooked and smoked thousands of game birds.

It is our greatest hope that this book not only motivates hunters to get out and experience the wonderful opportunities our planet has to offer, but to also appreciate the culinary delights game birds have to offer. Lean, organically grown, free-range, pesticide-free are all terms we hear when describing the ultimate meat protein sources. Wild game birds offer all of the above.

Just like any other animal protein source, how birds are handled prior to consumption can make a big difference in their overall flavor. Be sure and read through the appendix of this book for valuable information on proper handling–cleaning, skinning/plucking, aging–of all types of game birds.

Game birds should not be treated like store-bought chicken or turkey, as most wild birds are incredibly lean and must be cooked, accordingly. This book contains many suggested cooking methods for all wild game birds along with recipes specifically developed for each birds' taste.

Many game birds are interchangeable in recipes. More information on birds and portion sizes can be found in Appendix D. Game birds are seasonal and although we try to use them up while fresh, sometimes there are more than we can eat right away. Proper storage of game birds is important as many of the species have very delicate, easily freezer burned flesh. Smoking whole birds and making jerky is a fantastic, long-term storage solution and there is an entire chapter devoted to jerky.

The purpose of this book is to provide comprehensive guidelines that will take you from the field, through the handling processes and all the way to enjoying delectable recipes meant for wild game birds. We hope you enjoy it as much as we enjoyed creating it.

Wild Turkey

$\mathcal{W}$ ild turkey is healthier than domestic turkey, with more protein, less fat and less cholesterol. It can be difficult to roast a whole, wild turkey with the expectation that it will be like a round, plump, store-bought, holiday centerpiece. Contrary to popular belief, real wild turkeys are not shaped like a ball, nor do they naturally come with 3-5 pound breasts. They are however, delicious, full of flavor and easy to cook with. Most of the recipes in this chapter can be adapted and used for any upland game bird. Use the conversions found in Appendix D to help with exchanges.

Contents

White Chili

One of the most enjoyable elements of Tiffany's job is teaching cooking seminars. White Chili made with ground wild turkey or other upland game birds was developed for the O'Laughlin Camp Cooking Seminars in 2011. Hundreds of seminar attendees and sportshow vendors sampled this chili and the reviews were fantastic.

INGREDIENTS

- 2 tablespoons olive oil
- 1 cup onion, diced
- 4-6 cloves garlic, minced
- 2 pounds turkey, ground or finely chopped
- 2 teaspoons oregano
- 2 teaspoons cumin
- 1/2-1 teaspoon red chili flakes
- 2 7-ounce cans diced green chilies
- 1 tablespoon green Tabasco sauce
- 6 cups turkey/chicken stock or broth
- 3 15-ounce cans cannellini or white beans
- 1 cup instant or real mashed potatoes
- Salt & pepper to taste
- Juice of 1 lime

In a large pot, saute onion and garlic in olive oil on medium heat, 2-3 minutes. Add turkey and seasonings, sauteing an additional 5 minutes. Add remaining ingredients, except lime juice, and simmer at least 30 minutes. Remove from heat, add lime juice and serve.

Indonesian Turkey Soup

Soto Ayam is the chicken soup cure-all of Indonesia. The first, and best, Soto Ayam we had on Sumatra (where we lived for four years), was from a Pekanbaru Airport vendor. We made it a point to have a bowl before every departure. Leftover, cooked turkey can also be used in this recipe.

INGREDIENTS

- 2 tablespoons olive oil
- 1/2 cup onion, chopped
- 3 shallots, sliced (optional)
- 1/2 cup celery, chopped
- 1/2 cup carrots, julienned
- 3 cloves garlic, minced
- 1" fresh ginger, grated
- 1 stalk lemon grass, bruised* (optional)
- 4 cups turkey/chicken broth or stock
- 2 cups turkey, cubed
- Salt & pepper to taste
- Cilantro for garnish

In a large pot, saute onion, shallots and celery in olive oil on medium-high heat until onions are soft. Add carrot, garlic, ginger and lemon grass (cut stalk into 4"-6" pieces) and saute an additional 2-3 minutes. Add broth and bring to a low-boil. Add turkey and cook until turkey is done, 15-20 minutes. Garnish with fresh cilantro if desired.

*To bruise lemon grass stalks, lightly pound with a mallet or the back of a knife until fibers begin to separate. Lemon grass should be removed from soup prior to serving.

Leafy Green Potato Soup

We all need to get more nutrient-dense, leafy greens into our diets. Not only do leafy greens offer significant amounts of vitamins, minerals and fiber, they are known to prevent many diseases. Whether it's spinach, chard, kale, mustard, turnip, beet or collard greens, soup is an easy way to bring more color into your food.

INGREDIENTS

- 2 tablespoons olive oil
- 4-6 cloves garlic, minced
- 3 cups red or white potatoes, cubed
- 2 carrots, sliced
- 4 cups kale, chard or greens, chopped
- 2 cups spinach
- 1 cup green onions, sliced
- 4 cups turkey/chicken stock or broth
- 1 cup white wine
- 2 cups turkey, cubed
- 2 tablespoons Dijon mustard (optional)
- 1/2 teaspoon cayenne pepper
- Salt & pepper to taste

In a large pot, saute garlic in olive oil on medium heat, 1 minute. Add remaining vegetables and saute an additional 2-3 minutes. Add broth and wine, bringing to a low-boil. Add turkey, mustard and pepper, cooking until turkey is done, 15-20 minutes.

Tortilla Soup

There are many varieties of Tortilla Soup out there. This is a quick and easy fix, especially if a few cups of turkey are left over from a previous meal. Our kids wouldn't try this soup until we nicknamed it "Dorito" Soup. Use prepared taco seasoning or make your own with 2 teaspoons chili powder and cumin and 1 teaspoon poultry seasoning.

INGREDIENTS

- 2 tablespoons olive oil
- 1 cup onion, diced
- 1 cup red bell pepper, diced
- 1 cup corn, fresh or frozen
- 2 cups turkey, cubed
- 1 1.5-ounce package taco seasoning
- 1 15-ounce can tomato sauce
- 6 cups turkey/chicken stock or broth
- 1 15-ounce can pinto beans, drained
- 2 cups crushed tortilla chips or
- 6 small corn tortillas, torn into pieces

In a large pot, saute onion, pepper and corn in olive oil on medium heat, 2-3 minutes. Add turkey and seasoning, sauteing an additional 5 minutes. Add remaining ingredients and simmer, 20-30 minutes. Serve with chopped avocado, sour cream, shredded cheese, a lime wedge and/or cilantro for garnish.

Note: Refried beans can be used in place of pinto beans or beans can be pureed prior to adding to soup.

Curried Turkey Salad

One of the most requested salads from my mother's kitchen, Curried Turkey Salad, was served at both of my baby showers and usually has a spot at the Easter Brunch Buffet every year. An exotic and versatile comfort food, this salad can be served over salad greens, put into sandwiches or served with crackers.

INGREDIENTS

- 2 cups turkey, cubed
- 4 cups turkey/chicken stock
- 1 1/2 cups red grapes, halved
- 1 1/2 cups green apple, chopped
- 1/2 cup slivered almonds
- 1/3 cup green onion or chives, finely chopped
- 3 tablespoons sour cream or plain yogurt
- 2 tablespoons mayonnaise
- 2 tablespoons milk
- 1-2 teaspoons curry powder
- Salt & white pepper to taste
- Salad greens

Poach turkey and cool completely–previously cooked turkey can be used in this recipe but it will not be as moist. To poach turkey, bring 4 cups turkey/chicken stock or broth to a boil. Add cubed turkey and reduce to medium-high heat. Cook 10-15 minutes. Drain and cool.

In a small bowl whisk sour cream, mayonnaise, milk and curry powder. Salt and pepper to taste. In a large bowl toss turkey, grapes, apples, almonds and onions or chives. Gently fold sour cream mixture into turkey mixture. Refrigerate at least 30 minutes before serving.

Chipotle Turkey Salad

Served over greens such as lettuce, spinach and/or shredded cabbage this salad makes a great light lunch or brunch meal. Ingredients can also be stirred into cooled pasta for Chipotle Pasta Salad.

INGREDIENTS

- 1/3 cup plain yogurt or sour cream
- 1/4 cup mayonnaise
- 2 tablespoons chipotle chilies, diced
- 1 tablespoon honey
- 1 tablespoon Worcestershire sauce
- 2 cups cooked turkey, cubed
- 6 cups salad greens
- 1 tomato, sliced
- 1 green bell pepper, sliced
- 1 15-ounce can black beans, drained
- 1 cup corn
- 1/2 red onion, sliced
- 1/2 cup queso fresco or mild feta cheese

In a medium bowl, blend first five ingredients. Add turkey, stirring to coat. Divide remaining ingredients among 4-6 salad plates. Top salads with chipotle turkey mixture and crumbled cheese.

Turkey Satay

You can't go wrong with meat on a stick. Across the world, this popular cooking method has an endless variety of flavor combinations. Put only turkey on the stick or add fruits and vegetables, customizing as desired.

INGREDIENTS
- 1 pound turkey breast

COCONUT MARINADE
- 1/2 cup coconut milk
- 2 garlic cloves, finely chopped
- 1/4 cup scallion or onion, finely chopped
- 2" freshly grated ginger
- 2 tablespoons fresh cilantro, chopped
- 1 tablespoon lime juice
- 1 tsp ground cumin
- 1 tsp ground coriander
- 1/2 tsp turmeric (optional)

- Bamboo skewers, soaked 15-30 minutes

Cut turkey into 1-inch pieces or 1/2" strips. In a large bowl, mix marinade ingredients until thoroughly combined. Marinate turkey up to 12 hours, refrigerated. Let meat sit at room temperature 30 minutes before cooking. Thread turkey pieces on to presoaked skewers. Discard remaining marinade. Place skewers on a hot, well-lubricated grill. Grill 3-4 minutes on each side or until cooked through. Serve with Peanut Sauce (page 123).

Egg Rolls

Known throughout Indonesia as Lumpia, these tasty treats are usually a part of every party or celebration. During Tiffany's years as a preschool teacher on Sumatra, every Tuesday, Lumpia was on the assigned snack menu. It was fun comparing all the styles and tastes of these mini-egg rolls the students brought in to share.

INGREDIENTS

- 1 tablespoon olive oil
- 1 pound turkey, ground or finely chopped
- 1/2 cup onion, diced
- 4 cloves garlic, pureed
- 1/2 cup carrots, grated
- 1/2 cup cabbage, grated
- 1/2 cup green beans, diced
- 1 tablespoon soy sauce
- Salt & pepper to taste
- 30 wonton, spring roll or lumpia wrappers
- Oil for frying

In a large skillet, saute turkey in olive oil on medium-high heat until it is no longer pink. Remove turkey from pan and set aside. Saute onion and garlic 1-2 minutes until onions are soft. Add carrots, cabbage and green beans. Saute 2-3 more minutes. Add cooked turkey back into mixture and set aside until cool enough to handle.

Lay wrappers on a flat surface. Place 1-2 tablespoons filling in the corner of the wrapper. Fold corner over filling, roll and tuck in the other corners. Roll the wrapper tight and seal with a bit of water. Keep rolls covered in plastic wrap until ready to fry.

In a large skillet, heat 1/3"-1/2" inch of oil until hot, 350°-375°. Add 4-6 rolls to the skillet and fry until golden brown on all sides (1-2 minutes). Drain rolls on a wire rack. Serve with Soy Dipping Sauce, Sweet Chili Sauce or Chinese Mustard.

Baked Turkey Patties

Super lean and packed with flavor, these patties can be made ahead of time and served as a breakfast in a bun or with White Gravy (page 129) on biscuits.

INGREDIENTS

- 1/2 pound turkey, ground or finely chopped
- 2 teaspoons olive oil
- 1 cup spinach, finely chopped
- 3 cloves garlic, minced
- 1/4 cup fresh parsley, finely chopped
- 1 green onion, finely sliced
- 1/2 cup bread crumbs
- 1/2 cup parmesan cheese
- 2 eggs, beaten
- 1/2 teaspoon salt
- 1/4 teaspoon white pepper

Heat oil in a large skillet, brown turkey on medium-heat. Remove from heat and add remaining ingredients, saving the beaten eggs to add last, after mixture has cooled.

Form the mixture into patties, small or bite-sized for appetizers, larger for a main course entree. Place patties on a greased baking sheet and bake in a preheated, 375° oven, 10-15 minutes.

Cherry Pecan Bites

Freshly made sausage with wild game is a great way to add moisture and flavor to meat. Ingredient variations are endless and any kind of upland game bird or waterfowl makes a great sausage.

INGREDIENTS

- 1/2 cup pecans, ground
- 1 cup instant mashed potatoes
- 1 pound turkey, ground
- 1/2 cup onions, minced
- 2/3 cup cherries, pitted and chopped
- 2 tablespoons olive oil
- 1 tablespoon parsley or cilantro, chopped
- 1 teaspoon poultry seasoning
- Salt and pepper to taste

In a small bowl mix pecans and instant mashed potatoes, set aside. In a large bowl mix remaining ingredients until thoroughly combined.

Form the meat mixture into patties, small or bite-sized for appetizers, larger for main course entree. Coat both sides of the patties in the pecan/potato mixture. Fry on medium-high heat in a large skillet, 3-4 minutes per side. Serve with Cran-Cherry Pecan Chutney (page 127).

Stuffed Turkey Meatloaf

Nothing says comfort food like meatloaf. Given the fact this versatile creation lends itself to experimentation, it's easy to find a recipe that pleases everyone. Adding eggs and oatmeal or breadcrumbs ensures the meatloaf will stand up to slicing.

MEATLOAF
- 1 1/2 pounds turkey, ground
- 1/2 cup onion, finely chopped
- 1 egg
- 1/2 cup oatmeal or breadcrumbs
- 1/4 cup parsley, chopped
- 2 tablespoons Worcestershire sauce
- 1 teaspoon salt
- 1/2 teaspoon pepper
- Zest from 1/2 lemon

STUFFING
- 2 cups packed spinach, steamed and squeezed dry
- 6 slices bacon, diced
- 1/2 cup roasted red peppers, diced
- 2/3 cup feta cheese, crumbled
- 3 hard boiled eggs, whole

- 1/2 cup ketchup for the top

In a large bowl, mix all meatloaf ingredients until thoroughly combined. In a medium bowl, mix all stuffing ingredients except the hard boiled eggs. On a large baking sheet spread out 1/2 of the meatloaf mixture to 1" thickness. Place filling down the middle of the flattened meatloaf, placing eggs in a line along the center of the filling. Carefully top with remaining meatloaf mixture, sealing the edges all the way around. Top with ketchup and bake in a preheated, 375° oven, 1 hour or until internal thermometer reads 165°.

Turkey Marsala

An amazing flavor combination, this recipe pairs incredibly well with any upland game birds. One bite and we're transported to a cafe in Rome where we first enjoyed this dish with a crisp, Italian chardonnay. Serve over a bed of buttery pasta or mashed potatoes.

INGREDIENTS

- 1 turkey breast, boned & skinned
- 1/4 cup flour
- 1/2 teaspoon salt
- 1/4 teaspoon fresh ground black pepper
- 1/2 teaspoon dried oregano or Italian seasoning
- 4 tablespoons olive oil
- 2 cups sliced mushrooms
- 3/4 cup Marsala wine
- 1/4 cup turkey/chicken stock or broth
- Juice from 1/2 lemon
- 4 tablespoons butter, optional

Cut turkey breast into 6-8 portions and pound to 1/2" thick. In a shallow dish or bowl, mix together flour and spices. Coat turkey pieces in flour mixture. In a large skillet, heat olive oil over medium heat. Place turkey in the pan and lightly brown on both sides. Remove turkey from pan and set aside. Saute mushrooms, 2-3 minutes. Add wine, broth and lemon juice to pan and stir well, removing all the browned bits from the bottom. Once liquid has thickened, add butter if desired. Add turkey back to pan and simmer an additional 10-20 minutes or until turkey is tender.

Tandoori Turkey

Wonderful served with spicy lentils and cucumber raita, Tandoori Marinade is a flavorful and tenderizing marinade that also works well with smaller, whole upland birds.

INGREDIENTS
- 1 pound turkey breast steaks

TANDOORI MARINADE
- 1 cup yogurt
- 2 tablespoons olive oil
- 1 tablespoon lemon juice
- 2 teaspoons vinegar
- 4 cloves garlic, crushed
- 2-3" fresh ginger, sliced
- 1 teaspoon coriander
- 1 teaspoon cumin
- 1/2 teaspoon salt
- 1/4 teaspoon cloves

Cut turkey into 1/2" steaks. In a large bowl, mix marinade ingredients until thoroughly combined. Marinate turkey breast steaks up to 12 hours, refrigerated. Let meat sit at room temperature 30 minutes before cooking. On a hot, well-lubricated grill, cook only until grill marks appear, 2-3 minutes per side. Steaks are thin and lean so they will grill quickly. Steaks can also be fried in olive oil on medium-high heat in a large skillet 5-6 minutes per side.

Turkey Tangine

*The joys of sweet and savory, crunchy and soft all come together in this Moroccan stew.
Couscous is the suggested side, but rice, noodles or potatoes can also accompany this dish.*

INGREDIENTS

- 1 turkey breast, cubed
- 2 tablespoons olive oil
- 1 cup onion, chopped
- 4 cloves garlic, minced
- 1 teaspoon lemon zest
- 1 teaspoon turmeric
- 1 teaspoon cumin
- 1/2 teaspoon ginger
- 1/4 teaspoon cinnamon
- 1/4 teaspoon allspice
- 1/4 teaspoon salt
- 1 15.5-ounce can garbanzo beans
- 1/2 cup dried apricots, sliced
- 1/2 cup almonds
- 3 small zucchini, thickly sliced
- 3 cups turkey/chicken broth or stock
- Salt & pepper to taste

Lightly season turkey with salt and pepper. In a large skillet, heat olive oil on medium-high heat. Add meat and brown on all sides. Add onion and garlic and continue to sauté 2-3 minutes. Add remaining ingredients and transfer to a tangine or covered baking dish. Bake at 350º, 45-50 minutes or until meat is tender. Serve over couscous.

Note: Alternate cooking methods are a slow simmer on the stove, in a covered pan or in a crock pot, 3-4 hours.

Red Enchiladas

For us, enchiladas are a recipe that changes with what is in the pantry. Fortunately, it seems you can add just about anything to this recipe and it always turns out great. Try substituting salsa or green enchilada sauce for red; or the creamy condensed soup for the yogurt. Cheddar or Monterey Jack cheese can be added if desired and spinach or bell peppers are nice, in the tortilla as well.

INGREDIENTS

- 3 cups cooked turkey, shredded or diced
- 1 cup plain yogurt or sour cream
- 1 cup queso fresco, ricotta or cottage cheese
- 1 4-ounce can diced green chilies
- 1 16-ounce can refried beans
- 1 6-ounce can olives
- 1 1/2 cups turkey/chicken stock or broth
- 1 19-ounce can red enchilada sauce
- 10-12 corn tortillas

In a small bowl mix yogurt or sour cream with cheese and chilies. Place 2/3 cup enchilada sauce in the bottom of a 9" x 13" casserole dish. For each tortilla, spread a heaping tablespoon of refried beans, 1/4 cup turkey and 2 tablespoons of the cheese mixture and fold in half. Place in casserole dish and repeat with remaining tortillas. Pour remaining enchilada sauce and turkey broth over enchiladas and sprinkle with olives. Top with additional cheese if desired. Bake in a preheated, 350° oven, 35-45 minutes.

The following stock recipes are simply a guideline; use what you have and feel free to experiment with flavors.

Basic Game Bird Stock

- 4-6 pounds bone-in bird pieces (cooked, smoked or raw)
- 3 onions, skin on
- 6 carrots
- 5 celery stalks
- 6-8 cloves garlic

Asian Stock

- 4-6 pounds bone-in bird pieces (cooked, smoked or raw)
- 3 onions, skin on
- 5 shallots
- 6 carrots
- 3" ginger
- 12" lemon grass (optional)
- 4 Thai peppers or 1 tablespoon red chili flakes
- 1 orange or lemon
- 12 peppercorns

Italian Stock

- 4-6 pounds bone-in bird pieces (cooked or raw)
- 3 red onions, sliced
- 2 green bell peppers, chopped
- 10 cloves garlic, smashed
- 3 sprigs rosemary
- 1/2 cup fresh thyme or 2 tablespoons dried
- 1/2 cup fresh oregano or 1 tablespoon dried

Add all ingredients to the pot with the carcass, salt and pepper to taste, fill the pot with water and simmer for 6-8 hours. For condensed stock, let the water boil down (this is nice for freezing as it saves space). For ready-to-use stock, add water a few times while simmering.

After stock has simmered, strain and discard all bones and vegetables. Stock is ready to use or freeze. See Appendix E (page 146) for more information.

Jambalaya

One of those throw everything in the pot type meals, Jambalaya, can be suited for any taste. For a milder version, cut down on the pepper. For more spice, add a few diced jalapeño peppers.

INGREDIENTS

- 1 pound turkey, cubed
- 1/4 pound bacon, chopped
- 1/2 pound chorizo or Andouille sausage, chopped
- 1 cup onion, chopped
- 1 cup bell pepper, chopped
- 1 cup celery, chopped
- 6 cloves garlic, minced
- 2 cans tomato paste
- 1 tablespoon brown sugar
- 2 teaspoons cayenne pepper
- 1 teaspoon black pepper
- 1 teaspoon white pepper
- 1 teaspoon ground oregano
- 1/2 teaspoon dried thyme
- 6 cups turkey/chicken stock or broth
- 4-6 bay leaves
- 3 cups uncooked long-grain rice
- 2 pounds shrimp
- Garnish with fresh parsley and chopped green onion

In a large pot, cook bacon on medium-high heat until crisp. Remove bacon and add turkey and sausage to pot, cooking 6-7 minutes. Add onion, pepper, celery and garlic and saute until onions are tender, 5-7 minutes. Move contents of the pan to the outside edge, making a large area in the middle of the pan. Brown tomato paste with brown sugar in the middle of the pan, 5-10 minutes. Add spices and continue to saute, 1-2 minutes. Add remaining ingredients, except shrimp, and bring to a boil. Cover and cook over medium heat 25 minutes. Add shrimp and cook 5-7 more minutes or until shrimp turn pink. Remove bay leaves before serving. Garnish with fresh parsley and chopped green onion.

Walnut Parmesan Strips

It isn't just kids who enjoy a crunchy coating over meats. These flavorful strips stay moist while baking or frying. Substitute different nuts or add some spice to the mixture for your own custom creation.

INGREDIENTS

- 1 pound turkey breast
- 1/3 cup walnuts, ground
- 1/3 cup parmesan cheese
- 1/3 cup breadcrumbs
- 1 teaspoon granulated garlic
- 1 teaspoon salt
- 1 egg
- 1 tablespoon cold water
- Oil for frying, if needed

Slice turkey breast into 1/2"-3/4" strips, about 2" long. In between two sheets of wax paper, pound strips to 1/4"-2/3". Sprinkle salt and granulated garlic over turkey, let sit 15 minutes. Mix nuts, cheese and breadcrumbs in a small bowl and spread on a plate. In a medium bowl, beat egg and water. Dip turkey strips into egg mixture, then coat with parmesan/nut mixture. Place on a greased baking sheet. Bake in a preheated, 400° oven, 15-20 minutes or fry in olive oil on medium-high heat in a large skillet, 5-6 minutes per side. Serve with sauce of choice.

Onion-Potato Chip Strips

Coating any kind of meat or vegetable adds a fantastic texture and flavor-layer to the food. The French fried onions and potato chips give these rather decadent turkey strips an incredible flavor boost. Bake for a healthier alternative but fry for a crispy, crunchy coating.

INGREDIENTS

- 1 pound turkey breast
- 1/2 cup french fried onions, crushed
- 1/2 cup potato chips, crushed
- 1/3 cup flour
- 1 egg
- 1 tablespoon water
- 1/2 teaspoon white pepper
- Oil for frying, if needed

Slice turkey breast into 1/2"-3/4" strips. In between two sheets of wax paper, pound strips to 1/4"-2/3". Prepare three shallow dishes for the three-step process. In the first dish place flour. In the second dish, beat egg and water. In the third dish mix onions and potato chips.

One at a time, coat strips with flour, dip into egg mixture, then press into onion/potato chip mixture. Place coated strips on a greased baking sheet. Bake in a preheated, 400° oven, 15-20 minutes or fry in olive oil on medium-high heat in a large skillet, 5-6 minutes per side. Serve with ranch dressing or sauce of choice.

Turkey Cutlets

Make this meal quickly by using a favorite prepared spaghetti sauce for the marinara sauce or make the marinara sauce from scratch. Cutlets can be pounded and tenderized ahead of time and kept covered in the refrigerator between sheets of waxed paper. Also great with White Gravy or Turkey Gravy (page 129).

INGREDIENTS

- 1-2 pounds turkey
- 2 teaspoons meat tenderizer (optional)
- 2 teaspoons granulated garlic
- 1/3 cup lemon juice
- 2 eggs, well beaten
- 1 tablespoon cold water
- 1 cup Italian bread crumbs
- 1/3 cup parmesan cheese, finely grated
- 1 teaspoon fresh ground black pepper
- 3 tablespoons olive oil
- Mozzarella cheese, thinly sliced
- Marinara Sauce (page 121)

Slice turkey breast into 1/2" cutlets. Between two layers of waxed paper, pound cutlets to 1/4". Sprinkle cutlets with meat tenderizer and granulated garlic.

Prepare three shallow dishes for the three step process. In the first dish, squeeze lemon juice. In the second dish, beat the eggs with water. In the third dish place bread crumbs, parmesan cheese and black pepper. Place pounded cutlets in lemon juice.

In a large skillet, heat olive oil on medium-high heat. One at a time, take cutlets from lemon juice, coat with egg mixture, press into bread crumbs to completely coat and add to hot oil. Fry cutlets, 3-4 minutes per side. Immediately top cutlet with mozzarella cheese. Top or serve with warm marinara sauce on the side.

Turkey Cordon Bleu

As a young girl, Tiffany's first "fancy" cooking venture was Chicken Cordon Bleu. Although this recipe takes a few steps, the finished product is well worth the effort. To make things a bit easier, this dish can be prepared ahead of time and baked right before serving.

INGREDIENTS
- 1 turkey breast
- 4 slices smoked ham
- 4 slices swiss cheese
- 2 tablespoons Dijon mustard
- 1/4 cup white or whole wheat flour
- 1 egg, beaten
- 1/2 cup seasoned breadcrumbs

Cut turkey breast into 4 equal pieces. Place turkey breasts between two sheets of waxed paper. Pound with a mallet or heavy skillet until turkey is flattened and approximately doubled in size. Spread mustard evenly over each piece of meat. Place ham and cheese slices on each breast, leaving 1/2" at one end. Roll turkey toward open end and secure with toothpicks if needed.

For the next three-step process, prepare three shallow dishes. In the first dish place flour. In the second dish place beaten egg. In the third dish place seasoned breadcrumbs. One at a time, coat rolls with flour, dip into egg, then press into breadcrumbs. Place coated rolls on a greased baking sheet. Bake in a preheated, 375° oven, 25-35 minutes or until meat thermometer reaches 165°.

Korean Turkey & Cabbage

A prime example of putting an ethnic twist on good ol' fried meat. A great addition to this meal is a few tablespoons of Kimchee. This process using any marinade and vegetable combination gets a meal on the table fast.

INGREDIENTS

- 1-2 pounds turkey breast steaks or strips
- 1 tablespoon olive oil
- 4 cups cabbage, thinly sliced
- 2 carrots, ribboned
- Cilantro for garnish (optional)

KOREAN MARINADE

- 1/3 cup scallions or onions, thinly sliced
- 1/4 cup soy sauce
- 2 tablespoons sesame oil
- 2 tablespoons rice or white vinegar
- 1 tablespoon honey
- 3 garlic cloves, minced
- 2" fresh ginger, grated
- Freshly ground black pepper

In a large bowl, mix marinade ingredients until thoroughly combined. Marinate turkey breast steaks or strips up to 12 hours, refrigerated. Let meat sit at room temperature 30 minutes before frying. Discard remaining marinade. Fry in olive oil on medium-high heat in a large skillet, 5-6 minutes per side. Remove meat from pan and saute cabbage and carrots until tender, use additional olive oil if needed. Salt and pepper to taste.

Turkey Grill

Any kind of wild game on the grill can be tricky due to the lack of fat in the animals. The most important things when grilling are to keep the grill well-lubricated and not to overcook the meat. Marinated turkey steaks only take a few minutes per side and should never be cooked well done. Marinades/Rub listed will accommodate up to 1 1/2 pounds of turkey steaks. Marinate meat up to 12 hours.

WHITE WINE MARINADE
- 1/2 cup freshly squeezed lemon juice
- 1/2 cup dry white wine
- 1/2 cup olive oil
- 1 tablespoon chopped parsley
- 1 teaspoon grated lemon rind
- 3 cloves garlic, thinly sliced

BBQ RUB
- 2 tablespoons paprika
- 1 tablespoon white sugar
- 2 teaspoons black pepper
- 2 teaspoons salt
- 1 teaspoon chili powder
- 1 teaspoon onion powder
- 1 teaspoon garlic powder
- 1/2 teaspoon cayenne pepper
- 1/2 teaspoon red pepper flakes

TENDERIZING MARINADE
- 1/2 cup red wine
- 1/2 cup Worcestershire sauce
- 1/3 cup olive oil
- 1 onion, chopped
- 3 stalks celery, chopped
- 4 cloves garlic, crushed
- 1 teaspoon salt
- 1/2 teaspoon black pepper

Cut turkey into 1/2" steaks. In a large bowl, mix marinade ingredients until thoroughly combined. Marinate turkey breast steaks up to 12 hours, refrigerated. Let meat sit at room temperature 30 minutes before cooking. On a hot, well-lubricated grill, cook only until grill marks appear, 2-3 minutes per side. Steaks are thin and lean so they will grill quickly. Steaks can also be fried in olive oil on medium-high heat in a large skillet, 5-6 minutes per side.

Rosemary Brown Sugar Steaks

Talk about a game "tamer," this full-flavored marinade enhances anything from wild turkey to antelope to bear. An older bird can marinate in this for up to 36 hours. Younger birds will benefit from a 6-12 hour soak.

INGREDIENTS

- 1 1/2 pounds turkey breast

SWEET ROSEMARY MARINADE

- 1/4 cup real maple syrup
- 1/4 cup soy sauce
- 1/4 cup Worcestershire sauce
- 1/4 cup cider vinegar
- 1/4 cup brown sugar
- 1/4 cup olive oil
- 3-4 cloves garlic, crushed
- 3 sprigs rosemary

Cut turkey into 1/2" steaks. In a large bowl, mix marinade ingredients until thoroughly combined. Marinate turkey breast steaks 6-24 hours, refrigerated. Let meat sit at room temperature 30 minutes before cooking.

On a hot, well-lubricated grill, cook only until grill marks appear, 2-3 minutes per side. Steaks are thin and lean so they will grill quickly. Steaks can also be fried in olive oil on medium-high heat in a large skillet, 5-6 minutes per side.

Mediterranean Thighs

Characteristics of a Mediterranean-style diet include olive oil, lean meat and lots of vegetables. This flavorful dish is a healthy, low carbohydrate, quick meal that can be served alone or as a side.

INGREDIENTS

- 3 tablespoons olive oil
- 4 turkey thighs, boned
- 2 tablespoons flour (optional)
- 1 cup onion, chopped
- 4 cloves garlic, pureed
- 1 1/2 cup bell pepper, chopped
- 1 cup dry white wine
- 2 cups turkey stock or chicken broth
- 2 tomatoes, seeded and chopped
- 1 cup greens (spinach, kale or chard), chopped
- 10 green olives
- 10 black or Kalamata olives
- 1 tablespoon fresh thyme or 2 teaspoons dried
- Salt & pepper to taste

Cut thigh meat into 1/2" strips. In a large skillet, heat oil over medium-high heat until hot. Season turkey with salt and pepper and sprinkle with flour. Brown turkey in oil, remove from pan and set aside. Add onion and garlic to pan, saute 2-3 minutes. Add bell pepper and saute an additional 1-2 minutes. Add remaining ingredients and bring to a boil. Boil 3-4 minutes to reduce liquid. Add turkey to skillet, cover and simmer until turkey is tender or finish in a 350° oven 30-45 minutes.

Note: Breast meat can be substituted for thigh meat—reduce cooking time by 10-15 minutes.

Mexican Slow-Cooked Turkey

We've smoked, roasted, braised and stewed wild turkey legs and thighs. Many recipes, countless methods and one way to cook this flavorful dark meat still stands above them all–slow-cooking. Because turkeys spend most of their time running around on the ground, their legs and thighs are sinuous. Unless you want to spend a lot of time separating out all the meat from the tendons and ligaments, throw this part of the bird into the crock pot. The meat stays moist, absorbs flavors and becomes incredibly tender when cooked "low & slow."

INGREDIENTS

- 2-4 turkey thighs & legs
- 1 onion, diced
- 1 tomato, chopped
- 1-2 jalapeno peppers, diced
- 1 4.5-ounce can green chilies, diced
- 1 6-ounce can tomato paste
- 1 cup white wine or beer
- 2 tablespoons chili powder
- 2 teaspoons cumin
- 1 teaspoon salt

In a medium bowl mix all ingredients. Place turkey meat in slow cooker/crock pot. Cover with vegetable/spice mixture. Cook on "HIGH" heat 4-5 hours or until meat falls from bone. Remove bones, tendons and ligaments (careful, some are quite small) and use meat for burritos, tacos, enchiladas or sandwiches.

Cranberry Apricot Turkey Roll

This is a fantastic way to enjoy the flavors of wild turkey. Sliced, this can feed many people and makes a great addition to a brunch or a light dinner. For a special treat, serve with Raspberry Sauce (pg 123), Basil Pesto (pg 128) or Turkey Gravy (page 129).

INGREDIENTS

- 2 turkey breasts
- 1 tablespoon olive oil
- 1/2 cup onion, thinly sliced
- 1/2 cup celery, diced
- 2/3 cup dried cranberries
- 1/4 cup parmesan cheese, grated
- 1 1/2 cups bread crumbs
- 1 cup turkey/chicken stock or broth
- 1 tablespoon fresh sage, chopped or 1/2 teaspoon ground
- 1 teaspoon lemon zest
- 1 egg, beaten
- 1/2 cup apricot jam or preserves
- 2 tablespoons olive oil (for brushing)

In a heavy skillet, heat olive oil on medium-high heat. Saute onion and celery until tender. Remove from heat and cool. Add cranberries, cheese, breadcrumbs, stock, sage, lemon zest and beaten egg. Gently mix until combined. Place turkey breast between two sheets waxed paper. Pound with a mallet or heavy skillet until turkey is flattened and approximately doubled in size. Brush both sides of the turkey with olive oil. Divide stuffing between both breasts. Fold over and place on baking dish. Cover the top of both breasts with apricot preserves. Roast in a preheated 325° oven, 1 hour or until meat thermometer reaches 165°.

Hungarian Turkey

Crock pot cooking makes most recipes "goof-proof." Taking the extra step to brown the turkey and onions prior to putting in the crock pot gives this dish a deeper flavor.

INGREDIENTS

- 2-3 pounds turkey breast and/or thighs
- 2 tablespoons olive oil
- 2 cups onion, sliced
- 1 6-ounce can tomato paste
- 1 cup turkey/chicken stock or broth
- 3 cloves garlic, pureed
- 3 teaspoons smoked paprika
- 1/2 cup sour cream (optional)
- Salt & pepper to taste

Cut turkey breast into 6-8 ounce portions. Generously salt and pepper turkey pieces. In a large skillet, heat olive oil on medium-high heat. Brown turkey pieces on all sides. Place turkey in crock pot. Add onions to the skillet and saute until tender. Add onions to the crock pot, scrape all brown bits into crock pot. Add all remaining ingredients to the crock pot, except for sour cream. Cook at high heat, 3-4 hours or until turkey is tender. Stir in sour cream 10 minutes before serving, salt and pepper to taste. Serve over rice or noodles, if desired.

Lemon Pepper Planked Turkey

Plank cooking is a "must-try" cooking method with fish and lean game meats. Not only does it keep the meat off the hot grill, but when the plank is soaked, keeps meat moist. Plank cooking is easy and if you haven't tried it yet, now is the perfect time!

INGREDIENTS

- 1 turkey breast (bone in or out)
- 1 chicken skin* or 1/4 cup butter, softened
- Lemon pepper seasoning salt
- 1 prepared plank (See Appendix F: Plank Cooking)

*Chicken skin or butter option: To keep moisture in game birds that have been skinned, some kind of fat must be added. One option that works well and has an amazing flavor is the skin from a domestic chicken. Buy a whole fryer and carefully remove the skin. Season game bird and wrap the chicken skin around the meat. Additional seasonings can be placed on the skin as well. An alternative method is to cover the turkey breast in softened butter before adding the seasoning.

Place seasoned turkey on prepared plank. Grill or bake in a preheated, 375° oven, 30-45 minutes or until meat thermometer reads 150°-160°.

Honey Mustard Planked Turkey Breast

Hands-down, our family favorite for wild turkey. This is the recipe to turn to when someone complains they don't like wild turkey—it's guaranteed to change their mind!

INGREDIENTS

- 1 boneless wild turkey breast (approximately 1 pound)
- 3-4 strips of raw bacon
- 1 prepared plank (See Appendix F: Plank Cooking)

HONEY MUSTARD MARINADE

- 2 tablespoons Dijon mustard
- 2 tablespoons rum
- 2 tablespoons honey
- 1 tablespoon olive oil
- 1 teaspoon coriander
- 1/2 teaspoon meat tenderizer (optional)

In a small bowl, mix all marinade ingredients until thoroughly combined. Place turkey breast in a sealable bag or casserole dish and cover with marinade. Marinate 6-24 hours, refrigerated. Place turkey breast on a prepared plank. Cover with sliced bacon. Grill or bake in a preheated, 375° oven, 30-45 minutes or until meat thermometer reads 150°-160°.

Sausage-Wrapped Whole Turkey

If choosing to skin a bird, special care must be taken when cooking to add a protective layer onto the bird or the meat will dry out before it is fully cooked. Making a "second skin" out of sausage will not only flavor the turkey, but it will keep the meat moist.

INGREDIENTS

- 1 whole turkey, cleaned & dressed (skin on or off)
- 1 1/2 pounds Italian sausage, ground
- 1 4-ounce can pimentos or 1/2 cup bell pepper, diced
- 2 teaspoons poultry seasoning
- 2 teaspoons salt
- 1 teaspoon pepper
- 2 onions, quartered
- 2 cups turkey/chicken stock or broth

In a medium bowl, mix sausage and pimentos until thoroughly combined. In a small bowl mix salt, pepper and poultry seasoning. Place turkey in a large roasting pan, sprinkle salt mixture in and around bird. Stuff onions into the cavity. Using the sausage mixture, form a "second skin" over the top and sides of the turkey. Pour turkey/chicken stock into the roasting pan.

Roast in a preheated, 325° oven, 1 1/2 hours, covered. Baste often, every 15-20 minutes. Uncover and roast until sausage browns and the breast reaches an internal temperature of 150°-160°. Remove from oven and cover. Let turkey sit 10-15 minutes before carving.

Roasted Turkey with Sage & Root Vegetables

With a thriving sage bush in our herb garden, we have access to fresh sage year-round. The perfect flavor for turkey, dried sage mixed with 1/4 cup of butter can be used in place of fresh for this recipe.

INGREDIENTS

- 1 whole turkey, cleaned & dressed (skin on or off)
- 2 baking potatoes, halved
- 1 sweet potato, halved
- 1 yam or parsnip, halved
- 3 stalks celery, chopped
- 25-30 fresh sage leaves
- 1/4 cup butter, softened
- 2 cups water
- Salt & pepper to taste

Spread root vegetables evenly in a deep roasting pan. Place turkey, breast-side up on top of the vegetables. Salt and pepper the cavity and outside of the turkey. Stuff celery into the cavity. Spread butter over the top and sides of the turkey and place leaves evenly on top. Add water to roasting pan.

Roast in a preheated, 325° oven, 1 1/2 hours, covered. Baste often, every 10-20 minutes. Uncover and roast until browned with the breast reaching an internal temperature of 150°-160°.

Remove from oven and cover. Let turkey sit 10-15 minutes before carving.

Note: To enhance moisture, this recipe can be done in an oven-safe turkey bag or turkey can be draped with a layer of cheesecloth (soak cheesecloth in water before covering turkey). Often, leg meat is very dry when birds are roasted whole. Throw them into a stock pot for some great turkey stock/broth, see page 23.

Brined Whole-Roasted Turkey

Brining a game bird is a great way to bring flavors and moisture into the meat. The chemical reaction that occurs during the brining process also helps to tenderize meat. Many flavors can be incorporated into a brine but the main ingredient is salt.

INGREDIENTS
- 1 whole turkey, cleaned & dressed (skin on or off)
- 2 apples, quartered
- 2 onions, quartered
- Olive oil

WINE BRINE
- 1 quart dry white wine
- 1 quart chicken broth
- 1/3 cup vinegar
- 10-12 cloves garlic, crushed
- 3 tablespoons salt

In a large bowl, mix brine ingredients. If the bowl is big enough to hold the turkey for brining, place turkey in brine or transfer brine to a large plastic bag and place turkey inside the bag. Brine, refrigerated, 12-24 hours.

Spread onions and apples evenly in a deep roasting pan. Place brined turkey, breast-side down, on top of the onions and apples. Strain brine and add 2-3 cups to roasting pan. Drizzle turkey with olive oil.

Roast in a preheated, 325° oven, 1 1/2 hours, covered. Baste often, every 10-20 minutes. Uncover and roast until browned with the breast reaching an internal temperature of 150°-160°.

Remove from oven and cover. Let turkey sit 10-15 minutes before carving.

Note: To enhance moisture, this recipe can be done in an oven-safe turkey bag or turkey can be draped with a layer of cheesecloth (soak cheesecloth in brine before covering turkey). Often leg meat is very dry when birds are roasted whole. Throw them into a stock pot for some great turkey stock/broth (page 23).

Bag-Roasted Turkey

Oven bags are a fantastic invention and work well with many meats. With the right amount of liquid, oven bags clearly help keep wild birds from drying out while roasting. When roasting a turkey, plan to put the carcass directly into a pot for turkey stock/broth; you won't be disappointed. Any unused veggies, stuffing and/or pan drippings help flavor the stock/broth as well. See stock recipes on page 23.

INGREDIENTS

- 1 whole or cut-up turkey, cleaned & dressed (skin on or off)
- 4 tablespoons bacon grease or olive oil
- 1 cup onions, chopped
- 2 cups celery, chopped
- 1 1/2 cups turkey/chicken stock
- 1 1/2 cups white wine
- 1/2 tablespoon salt
- 1/4 tablespoon pepper

- 1 large oven roasting bag

In a medium bowl, combine onion, celery and bacon grease or olive oil. Stuff turkey with mixture. Rub salt and pepper outside of turkey. Place turkey inside roasting bag. Pour stock and wine into bag and secure bag. Place 3-4, 2" slits in the top of the bag. Roast in a preheated, 325° oven, 1 1/2 hours or until the breast reaches an internal temperature of 150°-160°. Remove from oven and keep oven bag closed. Let turkey sit 10-15 minutes before carving. Discard onion and celery.

Deep Fried Turkey

Deep frying a wild turkey is a great way to quickly cook the bird without drying out the meat. Although it takes a lot of oil to cook it, the result is a super flavorful, moist bird. The oil is not absorbed by the meat, so it is not oily or greasy tasting.

INGREDIENTS

- 1 whole turkey, cleaned & dressed (skin on)
- 4 tablespoons Cajun seasoning (packaged or see Cajun Rub, page 124)
- 5 gallons peanut oil (see note)
- Long handled tongs
- Deep-fry or candy thermometer

Weigh turkey to determine deep-frying time. Dry turkey thoroughly with a clean dish towel and coat with 2 tablespoons Cajun seasoning. Pour peanut oil into a 10 gallon pot. On a propane cooker, bring oil to 375°. Using long handled tongs, carefully submerge turkey in the hot oil. Fry for 4 minutes per pound or until internal thermometer reads 150°-160°. Remove turkey from hot oil and place on a carving surface. Sprinkle with remaining Cajun seasoning and let sit 15-20 minutes before carving.

Note: To determine exactly how much oil is needed, fill frying pot with water first. Place unseasoned turkey in a clean plastic trash bag. Immerse bag in water letting excess water spill over the edges. Remove water 4"-5" below the pot. Lift turkey out of the water and note the water level. Discard water and thoroughly dry pot. Fill pot with oil to the last water level noted; that's the amount of oil needed to fry the bird.

Turkpheasquail

Though it wasn't easy to prepare, this is our favorite recipe in this book. Part of the challenge came when putting the birds together with the sausage, which is one of the best ways to keep game bird meat moist. Deboning each of the birds wasn't easy, either. Accept that it's a slow process, but remember that the final presentation is beautiful...and just wait until you taste it! This recipe carries a "wow-factor" people will be talking about for years, thanks to both the beauty and unique flavors.

INGREDIENTS

- 1 wild turkey, deboned
- 1 pheasant, deboned
- 1 quail, deboned
- 1 1/2 pounds country pork sausage
- 1 onion, chopped
- 2 carrots, chopped
- 2 celery stalks, chopped
- 2 sprigs rosemary
- 1/4 cup olive oil
- Seasoning rub of choice

See Appendix D for instructions on how to debone game birds. After deboning birds, lay each bird out butterfly style, skin-side down. Sprinkle seasoning over turkey and evenly distribute half of the sausage in a thin layer on top of the turkey. Lay pheasant, skin-side down over the sausage layer. Place remaining sausage on top of the pheasant. Place quail, skin-side down over the sausage layer.

Starting with the leg area of the turkey, roll up toward breast area. Pull both sides of the turkey in, like closing a book. Place roasting pan on top of the turkey and turn the whole thing over so the "seam" is down.

Place onion, carrots, celery and rosemary in the pan around the birds. Coat turkey with a light layer of olive oil. Sprinkle on additional seasoning rub.

Roast in a pre-heated 325° oven, 2 1/2 - 3 hours or until internal temperature reads 165°. Baste with pan drippings every 20-30 minutes. (Check temperature in several places to insure a proper reading throughout.) Let Turkpheasquail rest 30 minutes before carving/slicing. Turkpheasquail can also be braised, grilled or smoke-cooked.

Note: Many combinations of upland game birds and waterfowl can be used in this recipe. Bird breasts can be used in place of the whole, deboned bird (with the exception of the turkey, it must be used whole). For more information, see appendix D.

Phyllo-Wrapped Turkey

Since we're always looking for ways to keep moisture in our game birds, here is another method. The phyllo serves two purposes here—one is to keep moisture in and the other is to add an amazing "crunch" factor. With all those buttery layers, the phyllo pastry tastes great. See pages 107-109 for other crust ideas that can be used with turkey.

INGREDIENTS

- 1 whole turkey, cleaned & dressed (skin on or off)
- 1/4 cup butter, softened
- 1/4 cup butter, melted
- 8-10 cloves garlic
- 15 sheets packaged phyllo dough
- Salt & pepper to taste
- 3 potatoes, halved or a v-shaped baking rack

Place turkey, breast-side up, in a roasting pan or large casserole dish on top of v-shaped baking rack or in between halved potatoes. Pound garlic cloves flat with the broad side of a knife; there is no need to peel them. Fill turkey cavity with garlic cloves. Cover turkey with 1/4 cup softened butter and salt and pepper to taste. One sheet at at time, cover turkey with phyllo dough. In between each layer of phyllo, brush with melted butter. Turkey should have 4-5 layers of dough. Brush final layer with melted butter. Roast in a preheated, 325° oven, 1 1/2 hours or until the breast reaches an internal temperature of 150°-160°. Check turkey often and if phyllo begins to brown too quickly, cover lightly with foil. Let turkey sit 10-15 minutes before carving.

Smoked Turkey

Smoked game meats are at the top of our "favorites" list. It's flavorful, it's a great preservation method and smoked meat makes a tasty addition to any dish. Not only is the meat spectacular but the leftover bones make an incredibly smokey turkey stock/broth. Turkey breasts can be smoked in place of the whole turkey in this recipe.

INGREDIENTS
- 1 whole turkey, cleaned & dressed (skin on or wrap in cheesecloth)

BASIC TURKEY BRINE
- 1 1/2 cups brown sugar
- 1/2 cup non-iodized salt
- 1 quart water
- 1 quart turkey/chicken stock or broth
- 1 cup vinegar
- 1/4 cup garlic, minced

In a large bowl, mix brine ingredients until dissolved. If the bird has been skinned, wrap tightly in 1-2 layers of cheesecloth and secure. Fully submerge turkey in solution and brine 12-15 hours.

Remove turkey from brine and let "drip" dry. Do not rinse, discard brine. Place turkey on a rack to air-dry for 15-30 minutes (placing wet birds in the smoker can make a mess and lead to "off" smoke flavors).

Place turkey in a preheated smoker (160°F-200°F). Smoke 5-6 hours depending on bird size and internal temperature (150°-160°). Turkey can be eaten directly from the smoker. To retain more moisture in the meat, place turkey from the smoker into a sealed container or baggie. Refrigerate until cool.

Smoked turkey can be eaten "as is" or added to a variety of dishes. The meat can also be vacuum sealed and frozen for up to 3 months.

Upland Birds

John Hinderman

*F*rom the "bite-sized" dove to the mature rooster pheasant, upland game birds come in many shapes and sizes. Upland game birds are some of the finest eating fare in the world of hunting. When properly cared for this flavorful, organic, protein-rich, low-fat meat not only tastes delicious but is incredibly healthy. Almost all of the recipes in this section are interchangeable. Use portion sizes found in Appendix D to help with exchanges.

Contents

Tom Kha Gai

It's a toss-up between soups. We can't decide if we like traditional Thai Tom Yum or Tom Kha Gai, better. In a restaurant, we usually end up ordering both. Tom Kha Gai, a creamy, coconut-based, spicy soup makes any game bird come out a winner. Shop your local Asian food market for most of the soup ingredients—it's worth the trip!

INGREDIENTS

- 2 cups turkey/chicken stock or broth
- 2" galangal root, sliced
- 2" ginger root, sliced
- 1 stalk lemon grass, bruised* & chopped
- 2 teaspoons sugar
- 6 kaffir lime leaves, bruised*
- 2 cups coconut milk
- 2 tablespoons chili paste
- 2 tablespoons fish sauce
- 2 cups bird meat, thinly sliced
- 8 mushrooms, sliced
- Juice from 1 lime
- 1/4 cup fresh cilantro leaves

In a medium pot, bring broth to a boil. Add galangal, ginger, lemongrass, sugar and kaffir lime leaves. Lower heat and simmer 5 minutes. Add coconut milk, chili paste and fish sauce. Simmer another 5 minutes. Add meat and mushrooms and simmer until meat is cooked, 10-15 minutes. Add lime juice and cilantro before serving.

*To bruise lemon grass and lime leaves, lightly pound with a mallet or the back of a knife until fibers begin to separate.

Indian Curry Soup

Fragrant and spicy is the best way to describe Indian cuisine. The deep flavors and cooking methods enhance any type of wild game. Look for Indian Naan (bread) in the freezer section of larger grocery stores or make your own buttery, garlic flat bread to go with this soup.

INGREDIENTS

- 2-3 cups bird meat, chopped
- 2 tablespoons butter
- 1 cup onion, diced
- 4 cloves garlic, pureed
- 1" fresh ginger, grated
- 2 teaspoons cumin
- 2 teaspoons paprika
- 1 teaspoon curry powder
- 1 teaspoon cinnamon
- 1 teaspoon salt
- 1 teaspoon black pepper
- 1/4 teaspoon cayenne pepper
- 6 cups turkey/chicken/vegetable stock or broth
- Juice of 1/2 lemon
- 1 cup yogurt
- 1/2 cup fresh cilantro, chopped

In a large pot, saute onion, garlic and ginger in butter on medium heat until onions are soft. Add remaining spices and heat until fragrant, 1-2 minutes. Add broth and bring to a boil. Add meat, lower heat to medium-low, simmering 15 minutes. Stir in lemon and yogurt right before serving. Serve with rice and garnish with cilantro, raisins, toasted coconut and/or chopped peanuts if desired.

Creamy Mushroom Soup

Smooth and creamy, this comfort food is a far cry from the condensed stuff you get in a can. Served with some light, fluffy biscuits, our family prefers this dish "Biscuits & Gravy" style.

INGREDIENTS

- 2 cups cooked bird meat, chopped
- 6 cups mushrooms, chopped
- 1 cup onion, diced or 2 large leeks, sliced
- 1/3 cup butter
- 3 tablespoons flour
- 2 cups turkey/chicken stock or broth
- 2 cups half & half
- 1/4 teaspoon nutmeg
- Salt & white pepper to taste
- 2 tablespoons chives, chopped
- 2 tablespoons fresh parsley, chopped

In a large pot, saute mushrooms and onions in butter on medium heat 7-10 minutes. Stir in flour, mixing until no lumps appear. Add broth and bring to a boil. Lower heat to medium, add cream, nutmeg, salt and pepper to taste. Stir in cooked bird meat and warm thoroughly. Garnish with chives and parsley.

Lettuce Wraps

A great appetizer or light brunch item, lettuce wraps have become popular with the low-carb cooking craze. These bite-sized finger foods are a delicious way to introduce people to game birds. To double the batch, add 2 cups cooked brown rice to the meat mixture, doubling amounts of oyster and soy sauce as well.

INGREDIENTS

- 1 pound bird meat, ground or finely chopped
- 1 tablespoon olive oil
- 2 cloves garlic, minced
- 1 3-ounce can water chestnuts, diced
- 2 tablespoons oyster sauce
- 1 teaspoon sugar
- 5 green onions, finely sliced
- 2 tablespoons sesame seeds
- 4-8 whole lettuce leaves

Heat oil in a large skillet, brown meat on medium heat. Add garlic, water chestnuts, oyster sauce and sugar and saute an additional 2-3 minutes. Remove from heat and mix in green onions and sesame seeds. Separate lettuce leaves (butter, Boston, iceberg or leaf lettuce all work well). Divide meat mixture evenly among lettuce leaves or serve a portion of bird mixture with leaves on the side, allowing people to make their own bite-sized wraps. Serve with soy sauce for dipping.

Rice-Paper Rolls

Vietnamese Rice-Paper Rolls are becoming more familiar in America. These versatile, round rice-paper sheets are available at Asian food stores and larger grocery chains. It only takes once to realize the filling possibilities are endless in these no-cook, clever, tortilla-like substitutes.

INGREDIENTS
- 2 cups smoked or cooked bird meat, shredded
- 2 cups cabbage, thinly sliced
- 1 cup spinach, chopped
- 1 cup carrot, ribbons
- 1 cup cucumber, sliced in thin strips
- 1 cup red or yellow bell pepper, sliced in thin strips
- 1 cup fresh herbs, chopped - basil, mint and/or cilantro

- 8-12 rice paper sheets

VIETNAMESE DRESSING
- 2/3 cup fresh lime or lemon juice
- 3 tablespoons fish sauce
- 4 tablespoons honey
- 2 tablespoons white or rice vinegar
- 3 garlic cloves, minced
- 2 teaspoons red chili paste or red pepper flakes

In a small bowl, whisk dressing ingredients until thoroughly combined. In a large bowl, toss all other ingredients. Add 1/2 of the dressing mix to the large bowl, reserving the rest for dipping sauce. Mix in dressing and set aside (this mixture can be kept refrigerated up to 6 hours).

Fill a large bowl half full with warm water. Add 1 rice-paper sheet and turn over and over until softened, about 20 seconds. Once sheet is soft, remove from water and drain on a clean kitchen towel. Place approximately 1/2 cup bird/vegetable mixture in the middle of the rice paper wrap. Fold the bottom of each rice paper sheet over the filling, fold ends in (burrito-style), rolling into a tight cylinder. Place rolls, seam side down, on a cutting surface. Once all rolls are assembled, cut to desired serving sizes. Rolls can be left whole, covered with a damp towel or plastic wrap and kept refrigerated up to 4 hours before serving. Serve with additional dressing for dipping.

Pheasant Musubi

Inspired by the Spam and Teriyaki Chicken Musubi we enjoy daily on our trips to Hawaii, Pheasant Musubi is a great way to make a little bird go a long way. We break all the rules of proper sushi making but there is something about the warm, tangy rice melting into the nori with the flavorful pheasant bite in the middle that makes this recipe a winner.

INGREDIENTS
- 2 cups pheasant, cooked
- 1/3 cup teriyaki sauce (page 123)
- 2 cups medium grain white or brown rice
- 1/3 cup seasoned rice vinegar
- 4-6 sheets nori seaweed wraps
- 1/4 cup fresh cilantro leaves or 6 cucumber strips
- Pickled ginger, wasabi and soy sauce for garnish

In a small bowl, mix pheasant with teriyaki sauce and set aside. (Raw pheasant can be poached or quickly sauteed in teriyaki sauce as an alternative.) Cook rice according to package or rice cooker instructions (if using brown rice, increase water by 1/2 cup to make it more of a "sticky-rice"). While rice is still hot, add seasoned rice vinegar, stirring gently but thoroughly. While rice is warm, spoon on to nori, spreading evenly to coat entire sheet (leave approximately 1/2" uncovered on both ends). Place about 1/4 cup pheasant down the middle of the rice layer and add 6-10 cilantro leaves or one strip cucumber. Roll up nori, squeezing firmly by hand or with a bamboo sushi mat. Set aside and repeat with another roll. Using a sharp, moist knife, slice in desired serving pieces. Serve with pickled ginger, wasabi and soy sauce if desired.

Stuffed Wontons

Upland game birds lend themselves particularly well to this appetizer as sometimes the meat is in very small pieces due to shotgun pellet removal. Any ground game can be used in these tasty, bite-sized snacks. It's another great way to introduce people to the flavors of wild game.

INGREDIENTS

- 1/2 pound bird meat, finely chopped
- 30-40 small wonton wrappers
- 1 tablespoon olive oil
- 1 cup celery, diced
- 2 cloves garlic, minced
- 1 tablespoon soy sauce
- 2 teaspoons toasted sesame oil
- 1/2 teaspoon powdered ginger
- 1 tablespoon white or rice vinegar
- 1/2 tablespoon corn starch
- 1 egg beaten, for egg-wash
- Oil for frying (olive, canola or peanut)

Heat oil in a medium skillet, brown meat in olive oil on medium heat. Add celery, garlic, soy sauce and sesame oil, saute until tender. In a small bowl, mix ginger and cornstarch with vinegar. Add to skillet and saute until mixture thickens. Remove from heat and let mixture cool. In a small bowl beat one egg.

To fill wontons, place one wrapper on a flat surface. Brush entire edge of wonton with beaten egg. Place a heaping teaspoonful of filling in the center of the wrapper. Fold over to form a half-circle and tightly crimp to close (get a good seal or filling will leak out when frying). Repeat for remaining wrappers/filling. Heat 1 1/2" of oil to 350° in a large skillet. Fry 1 minute per side or until golden brown. Drain on rack before serving. Serve with sweet chili sauce for dipping.

BBQ Hot Wings

Call 'em buffalo, call 'em BBQ, we call them finger licking good! We use game bird legs and thighs, but they cook up similar to a domestic chicken wing. Many times we package and cook our game bird breasts separately from the legs and thighs. This is a great recipe for using up several batches of legs and thighs.

INGREDIENTS

- 2 pounds bird legs and thighs
- 3/4 cup flour
- 1 teaspoon granulated garlic
- 1/2 teaspoon salt
- 3 tablespoons olive oil
- 1-1 1/2 cups barbeque sauce
- 1 cup blue cheese, crumbled

In a small bowl, mix flour, garlic and salt. Roll bird pieces in seasoned flour. Heat oil in a large skillet, brown meat on medium-heat and place into an oven-proof casserole dish. Bake browned birds in a preheated, 400° oven, 10 minutes. Drizzle with barbeque sauce and 1/2 of the blue cheese. Return to oven an additional 10-15 minutes. Sprinkle remaining blue cheese on birds before serving.

Newbie Nuggets

Yes, birds have nuggets! One of our favorite ways to introduce people to the wonderful flavors of wild game birds is to shape them into nuggets. By combining game bird meat with chicken, the much needed fat not only flavors these nuggets but it keeps them moist. Occasionally, we enjoy these fried—"junk-food" style—but baked makes for a healthier alternative we often enjoy.

FILLING
- 1 cup bird meat, finely chopped
- 1 cup chicken breast or thigh meat, finely chopped
- 1 egg, beaten
- 1/4 cup parmesan cheese, grated
- 1 tablespoon lemon juice
- 1 tablespoon dried onion flakes
- 1 clove garlic, minced
- 2 tablespoons soy sauce
- 1/2 teaspoon hot pepper sauce

COATING
- 2 cups panko (Japanese bread crumbs)
- 1/2 cup flour
- 1 egg, beaten
- 2 teaspoons water

In a medium bowl, mix filling ingredients. Refrigerate at least one hour. Prepare three shallow dishes for the three step coating process. In the first, place flour. In the second dish, beat the eggs with water. In the third dish place the panko. One heaping teaspoon at a time, form meat mixture into a ball and press flat. One at a time, coat with flour then coat with egg mixture and finally press into bread crumbs on both sides.

To bake: Place nuggets on a greased baking sheet. Bake in a preheated, 350° oven 20 minutes. Turn nuggets and bake for an addition 5-10 minutes or until golden brown.

To fry: In a large skillet, heat 1/4" oil on medium-high heat. Fry nuggets, 4-6 minutes per side. Serve with ranch dressing, BBQ or honey mustard sauce.

Sesame Cilantro Chukar

Full of flavor and versatile for any game bird, the secret is leaving the meat in the spice paste overnight. Try this recipe with turkey breast strips or steaks, too.

INGREDIENTS
- 2-3 chukar breasts & thighs, skinned & deboned
- 1/3 cup sesame seeds
- Lime wedges

CILANTRO CHILI PASTE
- 1/4 cup cilantro, chopped
- 3 cloves garlic, minced
- 1 tablespoon sugar
- 1 tablespoon olive or peanut oil
- 2 teaspoons red curry paste
- 2 teaspoons soy sauce

Puree paste ingredients in a mini-chopper or food processor. In a large bowl, toss chukar pieces with paste and cover. Refrigerate overnight. Remove bird pieces from marinade and roll in sesame seeds. Place in an oven-proof casserole dish. Pour remaining marinade around the edges of the dish. Bake in a preheated, 400° oven, 25 minutes or until meat thermometer reaches 150°-160°. Garnish with lime wedges and additional cilantro before serving, if desired.

Thai Quail

The secret ingredient here is the fish sauce. Both fish and hoisin sauces can be purchased in the Asian food sections of almost any grocery store. Red chili peppers make a statement in this dish; ours were fresh from grandpa's garden.

INGREDIENTS

- 1 pound quail meat, deboned (8-10 birds)
- 1 red bell pepper, thinly sliced
- 3 hot chili peppers
- 3 cloves garlic, minced
- 4 tablespoons hoisin sauce
- 1 tablespoon Thai fish sauce
- 2 teaspoons white sugar
- 1/4 cup water
- 1/2 cup fresh Thai or regular basil, chopped

Heat oil in a large skillet, brown meat on medium-heat adding bell pepper, garlic and chili peppers after 2 minutes. Continue stir-frying 2-3 minutes. Add sauces, sugar and water and simmer 5 more minutes. Remove from heat and stir in basil. Serve over rice or grated cabbage.

Cashew Ptarmigan

Forget Chinese take-out, this quick and easy game bird version is fresh and delicious. If you haven't been far enough north to hunt ptarmigan, any other game birds will work in this recipe.

INGREDIENTS

- 1-1 1/2 pounds ptarmigan, cubed
- 1/3 cup flour
- 2 tablespoons olive oil
- 2 cups turkey/chicken stock or broth
- 2 tablespoons soy sauce
- 1/2 cup toasted cashews
- 1 teaspoon Chinese 5-spice
- 1 teaspoon powdered ginger
- Green onion for garnish

Dredge bird pieces in flour. Heat oil in a large skillet, brown meat on medium heat. Remove meat from the skillet. Sprinkle remaining flour in the pan and brown for 1-2 minutes. Add remaining ingredients and bring to a boil. Reduce heat to low and add browned meat back to skillet. Simmer 15-20 minutes or until meat is tender and sauce is thickened. Serve over rice or soba noodles. Garnish with sliced green onion, if desired.

Stir-Fry Noodles

A plate of noodles always finds its way to the table when eating any kind of Asian cuisine. These flat, lo mein or Cantonese-style noodles are very easy to work with and make a great one-dish-meal or side. Wide egg noodles can be used in place of lo mein noodles.

INGREDIENTS

- 1 pound bird meat, cubes or strips
- 1 cup onion, sliced
- 3 cloves garlic, minced
- 2 cups bean sprouts
- 3 green onions, chopped
- 8-10 ounces lo mein noodles
- 1 tablespoon olive or peanut oil

Stir-Fry Marinade

- 1 tablespoon olive or peanut oil
- 1 tablespoon soy sauce
- 1 tablespoon balsamic vinegar
- 1 teaspoon sugar
- 1 teaspoon cornstarch
- 1 teaspoon sesame oil (optional)

In a medium bowl, mix marinade ingredients. Add meat and let sit 20 minutes or refrigerate up to 6 hours. Cook noodles according to package directions.

Heat oil in a large skillet, saute onions and garlic on medium-heat 3-5 minutes. Add meat mixture with all marinade. Continue stir-frying 8-10 minutes. Add bean sprouts, green onion and cooked noodles, stir-fry until warmed throughout.

Smokey Paprika Birds

Rich and flavorful, the spices slow cook into these birds making them fork-tender, creamy and delightful. White wine can be substituted for the vermouth and plain yogurt will swap-out with sour cream.

INGREDIENTS

- 2 pounds game bird, dressed and cut in pieces
- 1/2 cup flour
- 1 tablespoon smoked paprika
- 1 teaspoon salt
- 1/4 cup butter
- 1/4 cup olive or peanut oil
- 2 cloves garlic, minced
- 4 shallots, finely chopped
- 1/2 cup turkey/chicken stock or broth
- 1/2 cup orange juice
- 1/2 cup dry vermouth
- 1/2 tablespoon paprika
- 1/2 cup parsley, chopped
- 1 cup sour cream

In a medium bowl, mix flour, paprika and salt. Coat bird pieces with flour mixture. In a heavy skillet or Dutch oven, heat butter and oil on medium-high heat. Brown flour-coated birds 5 minutes on each side in the hot oil and butter mixture. (This may need to be done in two batches.) Set browned birds aside. Add garlic and shallots to the skillet and saute 1 minute. Sprinkle remaining flour mixture into skillet, blending thoroughly with a whisk. Slowly add chicken broth, orange juice and vermouth, bringing to a low boil. Reduce heat to low, place browned birds and remaining paprika into the skillet. Cover and simmer 30-45 minutes or transfer to a crock pot and cook on high, 1-2 hours. Remove from heat, add parsley and sour cream. Serve over mashed potatoes.

Quail Fajitas

Great as a salad or main course with corn tortillas, Fajitas can be presented in a variety of ways. Pupusas or sopas (thick tortillas) are an interesting change and can be purchased or made from scratch (see recipe page 126). All colors of bell peppers and mushrooms are also great fajita additions.

INGREDIENTS
- 1 pound quail breasts, sliced
- 1 cup onion, sliced
- 2 tablespoons olive oil

FAJITA SPICE RUB
- 1 tablespoon chili powder
- 1 1/2 teaspoons cumin
- 1 teaspoon salt
- 1 teaspoon black pepper
- 1/2 teaspoon oregano
- 1/2 teaspoon paprika
- 1/4 teaspoon granulated garlic
- 1/4 teaspoon cayenne pepper

In a medium bowl, mix spice rub ingredients. Completely coat meat with rub and let sit 20 minutes or refrigerate up to 6 hours. Heat oil in a large skillet, brown meat on medium-heat adding onions after 3-5 minutes. Continue stir-frying 2-3 minutes or until onions are tender. Serve over pupusas, sopas or with warm tortillas and all the usual fajita fixings.

Jalapeno Bites

Whether fried, broiled or grilled, these tasty bites are irresistible. These can be made for a few people or hundreds. It just depends on how much quail you have on hand.

INGREDIENTS

For four "bites" you will need:

- 4 quail breasts
- 2 tablespoons cream cheese
- 1 large jalapeno pepper
- 4 slices thin bacon

Rinse each breast and pat dry. Cut jalapeno into fourths. Place 1/2 tablespoon cream cheese on jalapeno, top with quail breast. Carefully wrap bacon around quail and pepper. Secure with a toothpick if needed. Fry, broil or grill until bacon is crisp. Serve alone or on a bed of lettuce.

Bird Cacciatora

Made with guinea fowl from Africa, we've enjoyed this recipe on many safaris. One of many recipes we were eager to try out on our North American game birds, this dish didn't disappoint.

INGREDIENTS

- 2 pounds game bird, dressed and cut in pieces
- 1/4 cup olive oil
- 2 cups tomatoes, chopped
- 2 cups mushrooms, sliced
- 1 cup onion, finely chopped
- 2 cloves garlic, minced
- 1/2 cup red wine
- 1 teaspoon Italian seasoning
- 1 teaspoon salt
- 1/2 teaspoon black pepper

Heat oil in a large skillet, brown meat on medium heat and place into an oven-proof casserole dish. Add mushrooms, onion and garlic to the skillet and saute 2-3 minutes. Add remaining ingredients and bring to a boil. Pour everything from the skillet over the browned game birds, scraping all of the bits from the skillet. Bake in a preheated, 325° oven, 45 minutes or until meat thermometer reaches 150°-160°. Serve over polenta.

Chicken Fried Game Birds

Panko, or Japanese bread crumbs, are a cook's best friend when cooking for children. In our experience, anything coated in panko using the following process will be eaten by kids and picky adults, too. From bass and catfish to quail and rabbits, if it is fried using this recipe, there isn't a morsel left on the plate. Maybe we should try Brussels sprouts next.

INGREDIENTS

- 2 pounds game birds, cut in pieces
- 1/2 cup flour
- 2 teaspoons seasoning salt
- 1/2 teaspoon garlic powder
- 2 cups panko (Japanese bread crumbs)
- 2 eggs
- 1/3 cup sour cream
- Canola, olive or peanut oil for frying

Prepare three shallow dishes for the three-step process. In the first dish mix flour, seasoning salt and garlic powder. In the second dish, beat the eggs with the sour cream. In the third dish place the panko. In a large skillet, heat oil on medium-high heat. One at a time, take bird pieces and coat with flour mixture, then coat with egg mixture and finally press into bread crumbs to completely coat. Place coated birds on a plate so they can be added to the pan in large batches. Fry bird pieces, 4-6 minutes per side. Serve with ranch dressing, BBQ sauce or mashed potatoes & gravy.

Game Bird Gumbo

Dove, pigeon, grouse and/or quail all work well in this recipe. Gumbo flavors compliment the meat and the slow cooking process ensures tenderness. Although not listed in the ingredients, if you have file powder, sprinkle a bit on top right before serving. Made from the dried leaves of the sassafras tree, file is well-known as a finishing touch for gumbo.

INGREDIENTS

- 6 small game birds, dressed & quartered
- 1/3 cup olive or peanut oil
- 1/2 pound kielbasa, sliced
- 1/2 cup flour
- 3 cups turkey/chicken stock or broth
- 1 14.5-ounce can diced tomatoes
- 1 6-ounce can tomato paste
- 1 cup fresh parsley, chopped
- 1 red onion, chopped
- 2 cups fresh or frozen okra, chopped
- 1 yellow bell pepper, chopped
- 3 stalks celery, chopped
- 3 cloves garlic, minced
- 4 bay leaves
- 1 teaspoon salt
- 1 teaspoon thyme
- 1 teaspoon cayenne pepper
- 1 teaspoon black pepper
- 1/2 teaspoon allspice
- 1 tablespoon vinegar

In a large stew pot or Dutch oven, heat oil on medium high heat. Brown game bird pieces on both sides. Remove and set aside. Add kielbasa to the oil and brown 3-5 minutes. Remove and set aside. Add 1/2 cup flour to hot oil mixture, stir continuously until smooth and brown, 5-10 minutes. Slowly add broth, whisking mixture to prevent lumps from forming. Bring mixture to a low boil. Add 1/2 of the parsley and all remaining ingredients, including the birds, except vinegar. Cover and simmer on low heat 1- 1 1/2 hours or transfer to a crock pot on high heat, 3 hours. Add remaining parsley and vinegar during the last 5 minutes of cooking time. Remove bay leaves. Serve over rice.

Planked Pigeon with Pears

You may have tried it with fresh salmon on a cedar plank but if you haven't planked any game birds, now is the time to try it. Not only does it get the meat off of the hot grill but when soaked, the plank keeps meat moist. Birds can be seared on the grill then placed on the plank for the remainder of cooking time.

INGREDIENTS

- 3 pigeons, plucked and dressed
- 1 cup white wine
- 3 tablespoons olive oil
- 5 sprigs fresh thyme
- 1/3 cup fresh parsley
- 1/2 teaspoon salt
- 1/4 teaspoon pepper
- 1 pear, peeled and diced
- 1 small zucchini, sliced

- 1 prepared plank (See Appendix F: Plank Cooking)

Soak the plucked, dressed pigeons in lightly salted water, 1 hour. Rinse and pat dry. Place pigeon and remaining ingredients, except pear, into large sealable bag. Marinate 3-6 hours. Drain and discard marinade. Evenly distribute diced pears into body cavity of pigeons. Place sliced zucchini on prepared plank. Place pigeons on zucchini layer. Grill or bake in a preheated 325° oven, 30-45 minutes or until meat thermometer reaches 150°-160°.

Jalapeno Stuffed Snipe

Snipe hunting is a myth for some people but for wing shooters, it's fun reality. An elusive, seasonal game bird, snipe may be small, but they are tasty. The key is to cook them quickly with high heat.

INGREDIENTS

For each snipe, you will need:

- 1 jalapeno pepper
- 1 slice bacon
- 1/4 teaspoon seasoning salt

- 1 prepared plank (optional)
  (See Appendix F: Plank Cooking)

Rub each bird inside and out with seasoning salt or your favorite grill seasoning. Stuff whole jalapeno pepper, seeds and all, inside the cavity of the bird. Wrap the snipe tightly with bacon slice. Cook snipe breast-side-up. Snipe can be planked cooked in a 475° grill or roasted in the oven in a casserole pan (place 1/4 cup water in the bottom of the pan to keep the snipe moist) 10-12 minutes. Oven broiling or direct cooking on a hot grill is also an option. Broil or grill 4-5 minutes per side.

Hungarian Partridge in Wine

Tangy and buttery, this dish represents the French country cooking we enjoyed on our trip through Europe. This "low & slow" cooking recipe lends itself to any other upland game bird preparation.

INGREDIENTS

- 2-4 Hungarian partridge, dressed
- 4 tablespoons butter, divided
- 2 tablespoons olive oil
- 3 tablespoons flour
- 1/3 cup red onion, chopped
- 1 1/2 cups mushrooms, chopped
- 2 cloves garlic, pureed
- 1/2 cup turkey/chicken stock or broth
- 1 cup white wine

In a large skillet, heat 2 tablespoons of the butter and oil on medium-high heat. Salt and pepper birds inside and out. Roll birds in flour and brown on all sides in the skillet. Remove birds from pan and set aside. Add remaining butter to skillet and saute onions, mushrooms and garlic, 3-5 minutes. Add broth and wine and bring to a boil. Whisk constantly and let sauce thicken, 3-4 minutes. Add birds back into pan, cover and simmer until birds are tender, 30-45 minutes.

Lime Pineapple Quail

This quick and easy recipe combines the convenience of a store-bought sauce and the tangy flavors of the tropics. Serve as a bite-sized appetizer or serve several birds over rice for a meal.

INGREDIENTS

- 6-8 whole quail, dressed
- 1 20-ounce can pineapple chunks with liquid
- 3 tablespoons A-1 Steak sauce
- 2 tablespoons spicy mustard
- 2 tablespoons olive oil
- 1 tablespoon cornstarch (dissolve in lime juice)
- Juice from 1 lime
- 1 teaspoon red pepper flakes

Place quail breast-side down in a deep roasting pan or oven-proof casserole dish. In a medium bowl combine all other ingredients. Pour pineapple mixture over quail. Roast in a preheated, 400° oven, 20 minutes. Remove from oven, carefully turn quail over to breast-side-up. Baste thoroughly with pineapple mixture and return to the oven for 20 more minutes or until meat thermometer reaches 150°-160°.

Lemon Pepper Packets

An easy way to prepare one or several game birds. Packets can be assembled up to one day ahead. If headed to camp, assemble birds and place in a sealable plastic bag. When ready to campfire cook, empty plastic bag into foil pouch and you're set. This recipe also works well when using only breasts or only leg and thigh pieces.

INGREDIENTS

- 1 game bird, dressed
- 1/4 onion, chopped
- 1/2 stalk celery
- 1 lemon, sliced
- 1 teaspoon lemon pepper
- 3 sliced bacon
- 2 tablespoons white wine
- Salt to taste

Place dressed bird on a square of aluminum foil, breast-side up. Fill body cavity with onion, celery and lemon. Sprinkle lemon pepper and salt over bird. Lay strips of bacon over the breast, tucking extra underneath. Close packet leaving a small opening at the top. Pour in wine and seal foil closed. Bake in a preheated, 350° oven or medium-hot grill, 30-45 minutes or until meat thermometer reaches 150°-160°. Open packets slightly at the top to brown bacon during last 5 minutes of cooking time.

Flat Tuscan Quail

Flattened and weighted, these birds cook quickly on the grill or griddle. Any upland game bird can marinate in this simple marinade for up to 12 hours. If you can't round-up anything to use to weigh down the bricks, cooking them on a George Forman-style grill works great.

INGREDIENTS
- 6-8 whole quail, dressed

TUSCAN MARINADE
- 1/3 cup olive oil
- 5 cloves garlic, minced
- 3 sprigs rosemary, chopped
- Juice & zest of 2 lemons
- Salt & pepper to taste

Cut birds through the backbone and press as flat as possible. In a large bowl, mix marinade ingredients. Marinate birds, refrigerated, 6-12 hours. Remove birds from marinade and salt and pepper to taste. Cover bricks or heavy stones with foil. Place birds on a hot grill or griddle and place weights on top of them. Cook 15 minutes per side or until meat thermometer reaches 150°-160°. Serve with couscous.

Apple Cajun Birds in a Bag

We can't stress enough the benefits of cooking wild game birds in a cooking bag. Bags keep the moisture and flavor in, preventing birds from getting tough, dried-out and overcooked. Variations are endless and experimentation with flavors is fun.

INGREDIENTS

- 6-8 small game birds, dressed
- 1/4 cup apple juice or cider
- 1 tablespoon cider vinegar
- 4 cloves garlic, crushed
- 1 red onion, sliced
- 1 apple, quartered
- 1/2 to 1 tablespoon Cajun Rub (page 124)
- 1 tablespoon flour
- Salt and pepper to taste

- 1 oven roasting bag

Place onions, garlic and apples in oven roasting bag. Lay birds on top, breast side up. Add juice/cider and vinegar to the bag. Sprinkle birds with seasonings and flour. Seal bag and make several slits on the top for steam to escape. Place the bag into an oven-proof casserole pan. Bake in a preheated, 350° oven, 45 minutes or until meat thermometer reaches 150°-160°. To brown birds, carefully slice open the bag down the center, tucking into the sides of the pan during the last 10 minutes of cooking time. Remove from oven and let sit 10 minutes. Serve birds with gravy from the bag and garnish with additional onions, if desired.

Wine Bagged Grouse

A very quick, flavorful meal. Add fresh herbs to amp-up the flavors. Once the bones are picked clean, they make a nice soup stock.

INGREDIENTS

- 2-3 grouse, dressed
- 1/3 cup butter, softened
- 1 onion, sliced
- 3 cloves garlic, minced
- 2 lemons, quartered
- 1 cup dry white wine
- Salt & black pepper to taste

- 1 oven roasting bag

Place one quarter of lemon in each grouse cavity along with some of the onion slices and all of the garlic. Place remaining onions and lemons in oven roasting bag. Place the bag into an oven-safe casserole pan. Cover the outside of the birds liberally with salt, pepper and butter. Lay birds atop onions and garlic. Add wine to the bag. Seal bag and make several slits on the top for steam to escape. Bake in a preheated, 350° oven, 45 minutes or until meat thermometer reaches 150°-160°. To brown birds, carefully slice open the bag down the center, tucking into the sides of the pan during the last 10 minutes of cooking time. Remove from oven and let sit 10 minutes. Serve birds with gravy from the bag, as is, or thicken on the stove, "pan-gravy" style.

Herb Roasted Pigeon

This is a favorite fall dish to create when the herb garden is busting at the seams. Experiment around with different variations and be sure to use what you have on-hand. Thyme, oregano and lemon balm have made their way into this recipe when in season.

INGREDIENTS

- 2-3 pigeon, dressed
- 1 bunch parsley
- 4 sprigs rosemary
- 10-15 fresh sage leaves
- 2-3 cloves garlic, crushed
- Salt & pepper to taste
- Olive oil for browning and drizzling

Salt and pepper bird inside and out. Heat 1/4" of oil in a large skillet and brown birds on medium-high heat. Remove from skillet and stuff liberally with herbs and garlic. Place breast-down in a casserole pan and roast in a preheated, 400° oven, 15-20 minutes. Turn birds breast-side up, drizzle with olive oil and roast an additional 10 minutes or until meat thermometer reaches 150°-160°.

Grouse with Sausage

Roasting game birds can be tricky. Their small size and lack of fat makes it easy to dry out and overcook these birds. Adding a layer of fat is one quick remedy, especially when wanting to cook birds whole. This technique is successful with any type of upland bird or waterfowl.

INGREDIENTS

- 2-4 grouse, dressed
- 1 orange, quartered
- 1 onion, sliced
- 2-3 ounces sausage, per bird
- Salt & pepper to taste

Season birds inside and out. Stuff a few slices of onion and one orange quarter in each bird. Place birds in a roasting pan or baking dish, breast-side up. Flatten sausage as thin as possible and cover bird breast. Wrap onions under and around bird legs. Roast in a preheated, 350° oven, 40-45 minutes or until meat thermometer reaches 150°-160°.

BBQ Brined Pigeon

Brining birds hydrates the cells of the meat, infusing flavor and tenderness. Brining is the first step when smoking birds but brining before cooking can be just as beneficial. The birds in this recipe can be roasted or finished in a slow cooker.

INGREDIENTS
- 4-5 pigeon, dressed
- 1/4 cup butter, softened

BBQ BRINE
- 1 quart water
- 1/3 cup brown sugar
- 2 tablespoons salt
- 1 teaspoon granulated garlic
- 1 teaspoon granulated onion
- 1 teaspoon liquid smoke
- 1/2 teaspoon white pepper

In a large bowl, whisk brine ingredients until salt is dissolved. Place birds in brine so they are completely covered. Birds and brine can also be placed in a large sealable baggie. Refrigerate 8-12 hours, turning birds at least once during this process.

Remove birds from brine and empty all cavities of liquid. Discard brine, do not rinse birds. Place birds on a rack to air-dry, 15-30 minutes. Coat birds liberally with butter and place breast-down in a casserole pan. (If using a slow cooker, put birds in and cook 3-4 hours on high.) Roast in a preheated, 400° oven, 15-20 minutes. Turn birds breast-side up, brush with additional butter, if desired. Roast an additional 10 minutes or until meat thermometer reaches 150°-160°.

Roast Pheasant

Pheasant is such delicate meat, special care needs to be taken to prevent the bird from drying out. The bacon and basting liquid work together in this recipe to add both flavor and moisture to the pheasant.

INGREDIENTS

- 1 pheasant, dressed
- 6 strips bacon
- 1 orange
- 1 bunch cilantro
- 5 cloves garlic
- Salt & pepper to taste

BASTING LIQUID

- 1/3 cup sherry
- 1/3 cup orange juice
- 1/3 cup turkey/chicken stock or broth

Place pheasant breast-side up in a shallow roasting pan. Salt and pepper bird inside and out. Cut orange in half and squeeze juice over pheasant. Zest orange peel over bird. Place orange halves inside pheasant. Place 1/2 of the cilantro bunch and all of the garlic inside the bird. Tie legs together with cooking twine. Completely cover the pheasant with bacon. In a small bowl combine basting liquid ingredients. Roast in a preheated, 350° oven, 45 minutes or until meat thermometer reaches 150°-160°. Baste every 10 minutes with basting liquid, use all of the liquid. Let sit 10 minutes before carving. To make gravy, melt 1/4 cup butter in a skillet on medium-high heat. Add 2 tablespoons flour and whisk continuously until mixture begins to bubble. Slowly add pan drippings and continue to whisk. Bring to a low boil, add more broth or water if needed. Serve over pheasant, garnish with remaining cilantro.

Second Skin Bird

When looking at the many different ways to keep game birds moist, we thought we had tried them all until we ended up with a stewing chicken that needed to be skinless for a recipe and a pheasant that needed a skin.

INGREDIENTS

- 1 pheasant or 2 chukar/grouse or 3 pigeons or 4 quail, dressed
- Skin from one chicken
- 1 onion, sliced
- Salt & pepper to taste
- Olive oil

Salt and pepper inside and outside of bird(s). If cooking more than one bird, divide chicken skin into equal parts. Drape chicken skin over game bird(s) securing with toothpicks if needed. Place onions in a shallow roasting pan, placing bird(s) on top. Drizzle with olive oil. Roast in a preheated, 350° oven, 45 minutes or until meat thermometer reaches 150°-160°. Baste occasionally with pan drippings. Let sit 10 minutes before carving.

Whole Smoked Pheasant

Whole pheasants are not only easier to deal with in the smoker than traditional jerky cuts, but there is much less waste. Once the bird is smoked the meat can be cleanly picked off the bones. The remaining bones make an amazing, smokey-pheasant broth boiled-up with onions, carrots and celery. Adding a layer of cheesecloth helps keep moisture in, as would wrapping the birds in bacon before smoking.

INGREDIENTS
- 2-3 whole pheasants, dressed

BASIC BRINE
- 1 quart water
- 3 tablespoons salt
- 2 teaspoons granulated onion
- 2 teaspoons granulated garlic
- 1 teaspoon white pepper

In a large bowl, whisk brine ingredients until salt is dissolved. Wrap birds tightly in cheesecloth, if desired. Place birds in brine so they are completely covered. Birds and brine can also be placed in a large sealable baggie. Refrigerate 8-12 hours, turning birds at least once during this process.

Remove birds from brine and empty all cavities of liquid. Discard brine, do not rinse birds. Place birds on a rack to air-dry for 15-30 minutes (placing wet birds in the smoker can make a mess). Place birds in a preheated smoker (180°F-200°F). Smoke 4-6 hours depending on bird size and smoker temperature. Birds can be eaten directly from the smoker once they reach 150°-160°. To retain more moisture in the birds, place the birds directly from the smoker into a sealed container or baggie. Refrigerate until cool.

Smoked Pheasant can be eaten "as is" or added to a variety of dishes. The tender meat can also be vacuum sealed and frozen for up to 3 months.

Note: This method can also be applied to other upland game as well as ducks and geese.

Crusted Game Birds

Putting any type of crust around a game bird is a wonderful way to seal in juices and flavor. When putting crusts around birds, it is better that they have a seasoned rub versus a marinade as the crust bakes better if there is no added moisture. For crusted bird recipes see pages 107-109 in the waterfowl section of this book. Any upland game birds can be prepared in this fashion.

Waterfowl

Waterfowl are among the most popular animals to hunt in the world. Although higher in fat than upland game birds, wild ducks and geese are still considered to be a low-fat protein source. Their dark, rich, flavorful meat can be prepared in a variety of ways. The biggest mistake people make is wanting their waterfowl to "taste like chicken." Ducks and geese closer resemble venison in their taste and texture. Special care must be taken not to overcook these delectable game birds.

Contents

Portuguese Meatball Soup

Rarely do we mix our big game meat with domestic beef. If we want to make a burger-size patty or sausage, egg is typically used as the added fat/binder. Be it big game or waterfowl, meatballs are a bit tricky as they need fat to keep their shape. Here, full-fat ground beef helps these tasty duck meatballs stay together from the skillet to the soup pot.

MEATBALLS

- 1 cup duck or goose, ground or minced
- 1 cup ground beef
- 1/3 cup seasoned bread crumbs
- 2 tablespoons ketchup
- 2 teaspoons granulated onion
- 2 teaspoons granulated garlic
- 1/2 teaspoon salt
- 1/4 teaspoon pepper
- Oil for frying

SOUP

- 1/4 cup onion, minced
- 1/4 cup bell pepper, diced
- 1/2 cup tomato, diced
- 4 cloves garlic, minced
- 2 tablespoons olive oil
- 8 cups turkey/chicken stock or broth
- 3-4 potatoes, large cubes
- 4-6 cups kale, chard or spinach, chopped
- 1/3 cup cilantro, chopped
- Salt & pepper to taste

In a medium bowl, mix all meatball ingredients. One heaping teaspoon at a time, form meat mixture into a ball. Repeat, keeping meatballs close to the same size. Arrange meatballs on a baking pan, ensuring they do not touch each other. Bake in a preheated, 350° oven, 20 minutes.

In a large soup pot or Dutch oven, saute onion and peppers in olive oil on medium-high heat until onions are soft. Add tomato and garlic and continue sauteing 3-5 minutes. Add stock and bring to a boil. Reduce to medium heat and add potatoes, cooking for 15 minutes. Add kale, cooking for an additional 10 minutes. Add meatballs and cook until meatballs are warm throughout. Remove from heat, add cilantro and serve.

Duck Noodle Salad

The key in serving duck in a cold salad is taking care not to overcook it. Cooked quickly (7-10 minutes in a 400° oven or fried in olive oil on the stove top) to an internal temperature of 130°-150° ensures tenderness and a better flavored bird.

INGREDIENTS

- 2 cups cooked duck or goose, thinly-sliced
- 6 ounces glass or cellophane noodles
- 1/2 cup carrots, julienned
- 1/2 cup celery, julienned
- 1/2 cup bean sprouts
- 1/4 cup green onion or chives, chopped
- 1/4 cup fresh cilantro, chopped
- 1/4 cup lime juice
- 2 tablespoons soy or fish sauce
- 2 cloves garlic, pureed
- 1" ginger, pureed
- 1-2 teaspoons chili sauce
- 1 teaspoon sesame oil
- 1 teaspoon brown sugar
- Chopped peanuts and lime wedges for garnish

Prepare noodles as directed on package. In a large bowl, whisk lime juice, soy or fish sauce, garlic, ginger, chili sauce and brown sugar until sugar is dissolved. Add remaining ingredients and toss lightly. Garnish with chopped peanuts and a slice of lime, if desired.

Deviled Duck

Scott's mom made him a sack lunch throughout all of his schooling (including high school). He has fond memories of this sandwich along with fried venison sandwiches and salmon sandwiches. She always sent extras of this one so he could share with his friends or trade them for dessert.

INGREDIENTS

- 1 cup cooked duck, finely chopped
- 1/2 cup mayonnaise
- 1/4 cup bell pepper, diced
- 1/4 cup celery, diced
- 1 tablespoon green onion, sliced
- 1 tablespoon lemon juice
- 2-4 dashes green Tabasco sauce (optional)

In a medium bowl, combine all ingredients. Serve with any style of bread and a slice of tomato.

Waterfowl Pate

Another great way to introduce people to the flavors of waterfowl. This is a family favorite and a great use of leftover duck or goose meat.

INGREDIENTS

- 1 cup cooked duck or goose, diced
- 4 ounces cream cheese, softened
- 2 tablespoons green onion
- 1 tablespoon Worcestershire sauce
- 1 tablespoon port
- 1 tablespoon fresh parsley
- 1 clove garlic
- 1/2 teaspoon lemon pepper
- 1/4 teaspoon powdered ginger
- 1/8 teaspoon nutmeg
- Salt to taste

Combine all ingredients in a food chopper or processor. Blend until smooth. Garnish with fresh parsley or green onion. Serve with vegetables, crackers or baguette.

Zucchini Pepper Stacks

Quick and easy to prepare ahead of time, these tasty little morsels work well with smaller breasted ducks. Fillings and cooking methods can be varied to suit your tastes—bake, grill or fry them!

FOR EACH DUCK BREAST, YOU WILL NEED

- 1/4 roasted red pepper
- 2 3" slices zucchini
- 1 slice Swiss or provolone cheese
- 1 slice bacon
- 1/4 teaspoon seasoning salt

Rub each side of the duck with seasoning salt or your favorite grill seasoning. Place duck breast on a flat surface and stack zucchini, cheese, red pepper and another slice of zucchini. Wrap bacon slice around the stack so the end is on the breast side of the stack. Bake in a preheated, 400° oven, fry in a frying pan or grill until bacon is crisp and duck reaches an internal temperature of 130°-150°. Serve whole or cut into bite-sized slices.

Goose Schnitzel with Caper Gravy

Hands-down, this is the family favorite for ducks and geese in our house. The kids like it for the cooking method ("tastes like chicken fried steak, Mom"), we like it for the tangy Caper Gravy.

INGREDIENTS
- 3-4 skinless duck breast halves
- 2 eggs
- 1/2 Parmesan cheese, grated
- 2 tablespoons fresh parsley, chopped
- Meat tenderizer (optional)
- Salt & pepper to taste
- 1 cup plain breadcrumbs
- 2 tablespoons butter
- 2 tablespoons olive oil

CAPER GRAVY
- 2 tablespoons butter
- 4 shallots, minced
- 2 tablespoons flour
- 1/4 cup capers
- 1 1/2 cups beef broth
- 1/4 cup parsley
- 1/2 teaspoon white pepper
- Salt to taste

Between two layers of waxed paper, pound breasts to 1/4". Sprinkle duck with salt, pepper and meat tenderizer if desired. In a medium bowl, whisk eggs, cheese and parsley. Put breadcrumbs on a dinner-size plate. One at a time, dredge breasts in egg mixture and coat with breadcrumbs. In a large skillet, heat butter and olive oil on medium-high heat. Fry schnitzel, 3-4 minutes per side. Serve with Caper Gravy.

In a medium skillet, saute shallots on medium-high heat until soft, 4-5 minutes. Add flour and saute an additional minute. Slowly whisk in broth and add remaining ingredients. Simmer on low heat until thickened. This gravy is also excellent with big game.

Spicy Peanut Goose

Tested on several "non waterfowl eaters" this recipe changed many minds. With just the right amount of sweetness and tang, the Asian flavors compliment each other and the goose, superbly.

INGREDIENTS
- 1 goose breast, skinned and boned

SOY MARINADE
- 2 tablespoons soy sauce
- 2 tablespoons olive oil
- 2 tablespoons cornstarch

SAUCE
- 1/4 cup water
- 2 tablespoons soy sauce
- 1 tablespoon sherry
- 2 teaspoons red wine vinegar
- 1 teaspoon cornstarch
- 1 teaspoon sugar
- 1 teaspoon sesame oil

FINAL PREPARATION
- 2 tablespoons olive or peanut oil
- 2 tablespoons ginger root, minced
- 1/2 teaspoon red pepper flakes
- 1 cup green pepper, sliced
- 1/2 cup salted peanuts
- 1 8-ounce can sliced water chestnuts, drained

Slice goose into bite-sized strips. In a medium sized bowl, mix marinade ingredients. Add goose and set aside for 30 to 60 minutes, stirring occasionally. In a small bowl combine sauce ingredients, set aside. In a heavy skillet, heat 2 tablespoons olive or peanut oil on medium-high heat. Sauté ginger and red pepper flakes 1-2 minutes. Add goose and all marinade. Continue to stir-fry 3-4 minutes or until goose is browned. Add green pepper and water chestnuts, stir-fry an additional 2-3 minutes. Add peanuts and sauce, continue cooking until sauce is thickened, 3-4 minutes. Serve over white or brown rice.

Tangy Diver Duck

Tested on some of the least desirable eating sea and diving ducks, this recipe is a winner with any duck. Even those who are adamant about not liking duck find they can't get enough of this flavorful recipe.

INGREDIENTS
- 2 pounds boneless duck pieces
- 1/3 cup flour
- 1/2 cup butter
- 4-6 cloves garlic, minced
- 1 onion, thinly sliced
- 1 orange or red bell pepper
- 1 green pepper
- 10-15 sage leaves, chopped

TANGY MARINADE
- 1 cup red wine
- 1/2 cup red wine vinegar
- 1/4 cup lemon juice
- 1/2 teaspoon salt

SAUCE
- 1/3 cup A-1 Steak sauce
- 1/3 cup orange marmalade or apricot preserves
- 2 tablespoons red wine vinegar

In a medium bowl combine marinade ingredients. Marinate duck pieces overnight, making sure duck is completely submerged. In a small bowl, thoroughly blend sauce ingredients. Set aside. Remove duck from marinade. Dredge in flour.

In a heavy skillet, heat butter on medium-high heat until melted. Saute garlic, onion, peppers and sage 2-3 minutes. Remove from pan. Add floured duck to the hot pan. Cook just until browned, 2-3 minutes. Turn and brown an addition 2-3 minutes. Add vegetable mixture back to the pan. Drizzle sauce over duck and vegetables. Stir gently and turn off heat. Let sit on warm stove 10 minutes. Serve over soba noodles or rice.

No-Fail Waterfowl

As a young bride, my first attempt at crock pot duck happened to be with eiders off the north coast of Alaska. It wasn't until after Scott was telling a friend in the "Lower 48" he had just eaten the best duck of his life, that we found out that almost everyone below the Arctic Circle considers these sea ducks inedible. Skinning and boning the stronger flavored birds helps tone down the gaminess. This recipe proves that some of the tried-and-true ways of cooking game are still pretty tasty.

INGREDIENTS

- 4 duck breasts or 2 goose breasts, skinned and de-boned
- 1 10.5-ounce can cream of mushroom soup
- 1 envelope (1-ounce) onion soup mix

ANY OR ALL OF THE FOLLOWING:

- 2 apples, quartered
- 4 stalks celery, chopped
- 1 onion, quartered

Place all ingredients in a crock-pot or slow cooker. Cook on high heat until meat pulls apart easily. Roughly 5 hours for duck, 6 hours for goose. Remove apples, celery and onion if desired. Using a fork, pull meat apart and mix with liquid. Serve over rice or noodles.

Cherry Duck

Sweet apple and tart cherries compliment the rich duck flavor in this easy to prepare recipe. Stronger flavored ducks can be marinated in equal parts beef broth and apple juice, up to 12 hours in this recipe, or see Soaking Solutions (page 143).

INGREDIENTS

- 1 pound duck breast, chopped
- 2 tablespoons butter
- 1/4 cup onion, diced
- 1 clove garlic, pureed
- 1 tablespoon flour
- 1/3 cup apple juice
- 1/3 cup beef broth
- 1/3 cup dried cherries
- Salt & pepper to taste
- Chives for garnish

In a large skillet, heat butter over medium-high heat. Add onion and garlic, sauteing until soft. Add meat (drain and discard marinade if used) and brown. Add flour to pan and stir 1-2 minutes. Add apple juice and beef broth to pan and bring to a boil. Lower heat, add cherries and simmer 20-30 minutes or until meat is tender. Garnish with fresh chives if desired.

Teriyaki Duck

When the boys were younger they thought it was hilarious to call this recipe "Teriyucky-Ducky" even though they loved it. There are some great teriyaki sauces on the market that can simply be added to stir-fried duck. This recipe is one I grew up making, with our farm-raised beef. It works great on fowl, too!

INGREDIENTS

- 1 pound duck, strips
- 1 tablespoon olive oil
- 1 1/2 cup bell pepper, chopped
- 1/2 cup onion, sliced
- 1/2 cup pineapple chunks
- 1 tablespoon brown sugar
- 1 tablespoon flour
- 1/2 cup beef broth

SOY-BALSAMIC MARINADE

- 1/4 cup soy sauce
- 1/4 cup balsamic vinegar
- 1/4 cup olive oil

In a medium bowl combine marinade ingredients. Marinate duck pieces overnight, making sure duck is completely submerged. In a large skillet, heat oil over medium-high heat. Add onion and saute until soft. Discard marinade, add duck strips to pan and brown 1-2 minutes. Add flour and sugar, stirring 1-2 minutes. Add beef broth to pan and bring to a boil. Lower heat, add bell pepper and pineapple and simmer 15-20 minutes or until meat is tender. If sauce is too thick, add pineapple juice or broth. Serve over rice.

Orange Pomegranate Goose

Orange and pomegranate make a great combination in many things. We like them in anything from a quick bread to a salsa. The one trick to this quick and easy stir-fry is to slice the goose meat very thin.

INGREDIENTS

- 1 pound goose, thin strips
- 3/4 cup orange juice
- 3/4 cup pomegranate seeds
- 1/4 cup soy sauce
- 2 cloves garlic, pureed
- 1 tablespoon olive oil
- 1 teaspoon cornstarch
- Green onions for garnish

In a large skillet, heat oil over medium-high heat. Add goose strips and garlic to pan and brown 1-2 minutes. Add soy sauce and continue sauteing 1-2 minutes. In a small bowl, mix orange juice and cornstarch until cornstarch is dissolved. Add orange juice to pan and bring to a boil. Lower heat to medium, add pomegranate seeds and simmer until sauce thickens. Serve with chopped green onions over rice, if desired.

Duck with Wild Rice

Mostly a "comfort-food" casserole, this wild rice dish can be used with duck or goose. It can be cooked in a crock pot as instructed, baked in the oven in a casserole pan or prepared as a Dutch oven meal while camping.

INGREDIENTS

- 2 pounds boneless duck, cubed
- 1/3 cup flour
- 5 slices bacon, chopped
- 1 onion, finely chopped
- 3 stalks celery, finely chopped
- 1 carrot, thinly sliced
- 1 cup mushrooms, chopped
- 1 cup chicken broth
- 1 10.5-ounce can cream of mushroom soup
- 1 10.5-ounce can cream of celery soup
- 1 12-ounce can evaporated milk
- 1 cup white wine
- 1 cup water
- 3/4 cup uncooked wild rice
- 3/4 cup uncooked white or brown rice
- 1 cup spinach
- 1/2 cup fresh parsley, chopped

Dredge duck in flour, coating all sides of the cubes, set aside. In a large stew pot, brown bacon on medium high heat until crisp. Add chopped onion, celery, carrot and mushrooms. Sauté 2-3 minutes. Add floured duck and brown, 5-7 minutes. Add remaining ingredients except for the spinach and parsley and gently combine. Transfer to a crock pot. Cook on high 2 hours, stirring occasionally. Add spinach and parsley 10-15 minutes before serving.

Cheese Steak Sliders

A great recipe for any ducks or geese. The trick is getting the meat sliced extra thin—it helps to partially freeze meat prior to slicing.

INGREDIENTS

- 1 1/2 pounds duck or goose, thinly sliced
- 2 tablespoons olive oil
- Salt & pepper to taste

- 2 cups onion, thinly sliced
- 2 cups green pepper, thinly sliced
- 2 cups mushrooms, thinly sliced (optional)
- 2 tablespoons butter
- 1 tablespoon olive oil

- 4-8 slices provolone cheese
- 4-8 dinner or hoagie rolls

In a medium bowl, mix meat with olive oil, salt and pepper. Let sit to reach room temperature. Heat 2 tablespoons butter with 1 tablespoon olive oil in a large skillet on medium-high heat. Saute onions until they begin to caramelize, 4-5 minutes. Add peppers and mushrooms and stir, frying 3-5 minutes. Remove vegetables from skillet. Add meat to hot skillet and quickly stir-fry until cooked throughout, 4-5 minutes. Add vegetables back to pan and gently mix into meat. Place a cut-to-fit slice of cheese on each roll and fill with meat mixture. Serve with marinara sauce on the side if desired (that's how we liked them in Philly).

Beer Brined & Bagged Goose

Due to the lack of fat in any wild game, there is always an issue with delicate meat drying out. Two methods to add moisture to meat are brining and cooking in a roasting bag specifically designed for the oven.

INGREDIENTS

- 2 goose breasts, boned with skin on
- 2 cups beer
- 2 cups apple cider vinegar
- 1/4 cup salt
- 1/2 cup brown sugar
- 4 cinnamon sticks
- 10 whole allspice, crushed
- 1 tablespoon peppercorns, crushed

- 1 onion, thickly sliced
- 1/4 cup marinade, strained
- 3/4 cup beer
- 1 tablespoon flour

- 1 small oven roasting bag

In a large bowl mix beer, vinegar, salt and brown sugar until dissolved. Add spices and goose breasts. Make sure goose is completely submerged, marinate overnight in the refrigerator.

Place onions in an oven roasting bag. Place the bag into an oven-proof casserole pan. Put breasts skin-side up atop the onions. Strain marinade and add 1/4 cup to the cooking bag along with 3/4 cup beer. Discard remaining marinade and spices. Sprinkle 1 tablespoon of flour into the cooking bag. Seal bag and make several slits on the top for steam to escape. Bake in a preheated, 350° oven, 45 minutes or until meat thermometer reaches 140°-160°. To brown birds, carefully slice open the bag down the center, tucking into the sides of the pan during the last 10 minutes of cooking time. Remove from oven and let sit 10 minutes. Slice and serve with gravy from the bag. Garnish with green onions, if desired.

Coconut Curry Pasted Waterfowl

Slathering wild game in spices is a great way to give them deep flavor and keep the moisture in. This Indian-inspired dish produces a rich, creamy sauce and keeping it all in the oven bag insures a delectable end product.

INGREDIENTS

- 1 large goose or 2-3 ducks, dressed
- 1 oven roasting bag

YELLOW CURRY PASTE

- 1/2 onion, chopped
- 4 cloves garlic
- Juice and zest of 1/2 lemon
- 2 teaspoons curry powder
- 2 teaspoons coriander
- 1 teaspoon cumin
- 1 teaspoon salt
- 1/2 teaspoon white pepper

- 1 14-ounce can coconut milk

Using a food processor or mini-chopper, blend all curry paste ingredients until smooth. Place goose or ducks into an oven roasting bag. Place the bag into an oven-proof casserole pan. Coat the bird(s) with the curry mixture. Pour coconut milk in bag. Seal bag and make several slits on the top for steam to escape. Bake in a preheated, 350° oven, 45 minutes or until meat thermometer reaches 140°-160°. To brown birds, carefully slice open the bag down the center, tucking into the sides of the pan during the last 10 minutes of cooking time. Remove from oven and let sit 10 minutes. Serve birds over rice with curry sauce from the bag.

Clay Pot Duck & Rice

Malaysia was the first place we enjoyed the concentrated, caramelized flavors of clay pot cooking. Since then we've added a clay pot to our arsenal of slow-cooking gadgets. When cooking any game meats, slow-cooking is a favorite technique as it is one of the best ways to keep food moist. Clay pots can be used for a wide variety of other recipes; we even love how it bakes bread.

INGREDIENTS
- 2-3 ducks, dressed
- 2 cups beef broth
- 1 cup brown rice
- 1 10-ounce can Rotel (diced tomatoes and green chilies)
- 2 tablespoons onion flakes

First, be sure to read the directions on your clay pot cooker and follow them. Clay pots can crack if not handled with care. Place clay pot cooker and lid together, so you can fill them with tepid water, soak clay pot 15 minutes. Pour out water and add recipe ingredients stirring rice, onion and Rotel into beef broth. Place ducks atop rice mixture and cover with clay pot roaster lid. Place into a cool oven. (Never preheat oven before baking with a clay pot.) Turn oven to 400° and bake 1 1/2 hours or until birds reach desired tenderness or temperature, 130° - rare, 140° - medium rare, 150° - medium, 160° - well done. Once removed from oven, the clay pot ingredients will stay warm up to 20 minutes without drying out. Never submerge or rinse clay pot with cold water for cleaning.

Basted Port Duck

Basting is key when roasting game birds. This orange port mixture is perfect for keeping birds moist and adding flavor.

INGREDIENTS
- 1-2 ducks, dressed
- 1 large onion, quartered
- 1 orange, quartered
- 1/2 cup port
- 1/4 cup butter, melted
- Juice and zest from 1 orange
- Salt & pepper to taste

Zest orange into a small bowl. Squeeze juice from the orange into the same bowl and discard any seeds. Add the port and butter to the bowl and mix until thoroughly combined. Season ducks inside and out with salt and pepper. Stuff birds with orange rind and onion quarters. Place birds in a roasting pan or baking dish, breast-side up. Roast in a preheated, 425° oven, 25-45 minutes or until birds reach desired temperature, 130° - rare, 140° - medium rare, 150° - medium, 160° - well done. Baste every 10 minutes with port mixture. Let sit 10 minutes before carving. (For a no-baste option, add ducks and basting liquid to an oven bag and bake at 350°.)

Herb & Gin Duck

When preparing waterfowl, take into consideration the type of bird and what they may have been feeding on. Birds that have been feeding on any kind of sea life tend to be much stronger flavored. The intense flavors in this recipe will help equalize a strong flavored duck.

INGREDIENTS

- 2 ducks, dressed
- 1 large onion, quartered
- 1 tablespoon peppercorns or juniper berries
- 2 sprigs rosemary
- 1 bunch fresh thyme
- 1/3 cup gin
- 1/4 cup water
- 1/4 cup olive oil
- 1/4 teaspoon cayenne pepper
- Salt & pepper to taste

In a small bowl, mix gin, water, oil and cayenne pepper. Season ducks inside and out with salt and pepper. Stuff a few chunks of onion, peppercorns, rosemary and thyme into each bird. Place birds in a roasting pan or baking dish, breast-side up. Roast in a preheated, 425° oven, 25-45 minutes or until birds reach desired temperature, 130° - rare, 140° - medium rare, 150° - medium, 160° - well done. Baste every 10 minutes with gin mixture. Let sit 10 minutes before carving. (For a no-baste option, add ducks and basting liquid to an oven bag and bake at 350°.)

Apple Raisin Stuffed Duck

A great one-pot meal as the cabbage cooks perfectly with bacon and duck drippings. Unlike some stuffings, the apples and raisins can be eaten instead of discarded. These can also be roasted in an oven bag, just be sure to slice open bag during the last 10-15 minutes of cooking time to crisp-up the bacon.

INGREDIENTS

- 3-4 small whole ducks, skinned
- 2 apples, cored & sliced
- 1 cup raisins
- 3-4 bacon strips
- 6-8 cups cabbage
- Salt & pepper to taste

Salt and pepper ducks, inside and out. Evenly distribute apples and raisins in empty duck cavities. Wrap each duck in a strip of bacon. Slice cabbage into a Dutch oven or casserole dish. Place stuffed ducks atop cabbage layer. Cover and bake in a preheated 350° oven, 45 minutes or until birds reach desired tenderness or temperature, 130° - rare, 140° - medium rare, 150° - medium, 160° - well done. Let sit 10 minutes before carving.

Roast Goose with Cranberry Walnut Stuffing

Don't wait for a special occasion to stuff a goose. This works great for a plucked bird but in our family, plucked birds are hard to come by, as skinning is much faster (and a great excuse to use bacon).

INGREDIENTS

- 1 whole goose, skinned
- 3-4 cups white wine
- 1 tablespoon salt

- 2 tablespoons olive oil
- 1/2 cup onion, diced
- 1 cup celery, chopped
- 2 cups bread stuffing cubes
- 1 cup crumbled cornbread
- 1/2 cup walnuts
- 1/4 cup dried cranberries
- 1 egg, lightly beaten
- 1 1/2 cups chicken broth
- 1 tablespoon dried parsley
- 1/2 teaspoon poultry seasoning
- 1/2 teaspoon black pepper

- 6-8 slices bacon
- White wine for basting

In a kitchen size trash bag, marinate goose overnight in white wine and a tablespoon of salt. (Double the bag and place in a bowl in case of leakage.) In a skillet on medium-high heat, sauté onion and celery in olive oil until soft. In a medium bowl mix remaining ingredients except the bacon slices. Place goose in roasting pan, breast-side up. Stuff goose with stuffing mixture. Tie legs together with cooking twine. Completely cover the goose breast with bacon slices. Cook in a preheated, 400° oven, 25 minutes. Turn oven to 325° and continue roasting for an additional hour or until birds reach desired tenderness or temperature, 130° - rare, 140° - medium rare, 150° - medium, 160° - well done. Baste frequently with white wine and bacon drippings. Let sit 10 minutes before carving.

Peking-Style Duck

Peking duck is Beijing, China's most famous dish. The first time we ordered it in downtown Beijing, it was obvious we were unsure how to properly go about eating it. A crowd quickly formed around our table and through hand-gestures, we were instructed on how to pull apart the duck, wrap it in the pancake with a bit of green onion and dip it in the hoisin sauce. It is difficult to completely duplicate what you can get in China, but this recipe comes close.

INGREDIENTS

- 1 large duck
- 6 cups water
- 3" fresh ginger, sliced
- 1/2 onion, sliced
- 3 tablespoons honey
- 2 tablespoons white vinegar
- 2 tablespoons corn starch

Place clean duck on a rack in the refrigerator 12-24 hours. In a large pot, bring water to a boil. In a small bowl, dissolve cornstarch in 4 tablespoons water. Add all ingredients to boiling water. Stir at a high boil 3-4 minutes. Submerge duck in boiling water mixture, turning to coat/boil all sides for 10 minutes. Place duck on rack and allow to air-dry at least 2 hours in front of a fan. Roast duck, breast up, directly on the rack in a preheated, 350° oven, 30 minutes. Place a large baking pan of water in the oven to catch any drippings from the duck. Turn duck over and roast an additional 30 minutes. Serve duck with hoisin sauce, green onion and Mandarin Pancakes (page 126).

Boneless Duck Roast

As mentioned in the recipe for Turkpheasquail (page 43), deboning a game bird lends itself to a variety of cooking methods and stuffings. We highly suggest trying a Turducken (duck wrapped in chicken, wrapped in turkey) or Turgoosegrouse (grouse wrapped in goose, wrapped in turkey) at your next dinner party.

INGREDIENTS
- 2-3 deboned ducks
- 1-2 cups seasoned sausage
- 6-8 fresh sage leaves (optional)
- 2 cups beef broth

See Appendix D for instructions on how to debone game birds. After deboning birds, lay each bird out, butterfly style, skin-side down. Evenly distribute the sausage in a thin layer on top of each bird. Wrap tail-end up first and fold sides over. Lay seam-side down in roasting pan. Add broth to roasting pan. (If grilling ducks, secure with butcher's twine and omit beef broth.) Cook in a preheated, 375° oven, 1 hour or until birds reach desired tenderness or temperature, 130° - rare, 140° - medium rare, 150° - medium, 160° - well done. Baste frequently with broth/pan drippings. Let sit 10 minutes before slicing.

* If combining game birds, cook to an internal temperature of 165°.

Salt-Crusted Rosemary Duck

Always looking for interesting ways to cook game birds, a friend suggested we try a salt crust. What a fine discovery it was as putting a crust around any game bird literally locks in the juices, making for a delicious whole-bird cooking method.

INGREDIENTS

- 2 medium ducks, dressed
- 2 sprigs rosemary
- 4 cloves garlic
- 3 cups salt
- 3 cups flour
- 1 cup water
- 1 egg, beaten

In a large bowl, mix salt, flour and water until a stiff dough is formed. Add more water if needed. Divide dough into 2 equal parts. On a floured surface, roll dough out so it is large enough to fold over the whole duck. Stuff ducks with rosemary and garlic. Place duck on top of rolled crust, breast-side down. Fold crust over and lay seam-side down in a greased casserole pan. Repeat with remaining duck. Brush egg mixture over top and sides of wrapped ducks. Bake in a preheated, 350° oven, 75 minutes. Serve ducks in crust, break open and carve. Do not eat the crust.

Flour-Crusted Peppered Duck

Salt Crusted Duck was our first success but there was no stopping us; of course we had to try another method. Flour-Crusted Duck made a beautiful artisan-style presentation. The only disappointment was that you don't eat the crust. This meal is complete with a nice side of garlic bread.

INGREDIENTS
- 2 medium ducks, dressed
- 1 lemon, quartered

PEPPER RUB
- 1/2 tablespoon lemon pepper
- 2 teaspoons celery salt
- 2 teaspoons dry mustard
- 1 teaspoon granulated onion
- 1 teaspoon granulated garlic
- Zest of 1 lemon

FLOUR CRUST
- 5 cups flour
- 1 cup water

In a small bowl combine rub ingredients. Stir until thoroughly combined. Generously coat ducks inside and out with rub. Stuff with lemon quarters and set aside. In a large bowl, mix flour and water until a stiff dough is formed. Add more water if needed. Divide dough into 2 equal parts. On a floured surface, roll dough out so it is large enough to fold over the whole duck. Place seasoned duck on top of rolled crust, breast-side down. Fold crust over and lay seam-side down in a greased casserole pan. Repeat with remaining duck. Bake in a preheated, 400° oven, 1 hour. Serve ducks in crust, break open and carve. Do not eat the crust.

Pie-Crusted Italian Duck

Now this crust is quite edible, in fact our boys chose this "crusting method" as their favorite because they love anything sweet or savory, with pie crust. Just a thin slice of seasoned duck and a bit of crust made for a tasty and interestingly presented appetizer.

INGREDIENTS

- 1 large duck, dressed
- 1/2 onion, chopped
- 1 tablespoon olive oil
- 2 teaspoons Italian seasoning
- 1 teaspoon granulated garlic
- Salt & pepper to taste
- 1 prepared pie crust

In a small bowl mix oil, Italian seasoning and granulated garlic. Salt and pepper duck, inside and out. Stuff cavity with onions. Lay pie crust on a flat surface. Coat duck with seasoning mixture and place breast-side down on the pie crust. Fold crust over, pinching crust to form a seal where it comes together and lay seam-side down in a greased casserole pan. Bake in a preheated 375° oven, 75 minutes. Serve ducks in crust, break open and carve. Crust is edible.

Game Bird Jerky

The process of hot smoking meat is simple; the combination of heat and smoke breaks down the fibers within the meat while drawing out most of the moisture. The result is a tender piece of cooked meat, packed with flavor. The longer the meat is exposed to heat, the drier it becomes.

No matter what recipe you apply, the goal in attaining a well-textured piece of jerky lies in creating a balance between salt, sugar, smoke and heat. Adding other spices and flavors you wish the meat to carry, is also part of the equation.

Jerky makes an excellent snack food out of any wild game meat, especially waterfowl and select upland birds. Most commonly sold in stores using beef, making your own jerky is not only a great way to use game meat, it is inexpensive and you can control the cut and the ingredients. Processed, packaged jerky is often made from chopped, formed meat using "spare-parts." When you are making your own jerky, it's whole muscle, pure meat. Whether you like salty, spicy or sweet, there is a recipe sure to become your go-to smoking choice.

In our experience we've found more people are willing to try different types of game meat when made into jerky. For those skeptics who voice displeasures of eating wild turkey, geese and diving ducks, give it to them in jerky form and their mind may be changed. Kids love it, astronauts take it into space, it can be sliced thin and added to salads, soups or fried rice—jerky is a great protein option.

Part of almost every type of wild game that we harvest makes it into the freezer as jerky, birds included. Not only is significantly less freezer space taken up with dried meat but the convenience of this high-protein snack is unmatched.

The best wild game birds for making jerky are turkey, ducks and geese. Smaller and softer meated birds—like most upland species—are difficult to cut for jerky so those are best smoked whole. See the recipe "Whole Smoked Pheasant" (page 80) for step-by-step instructions on how to smoke whole game birds.

Once the birds have been smoked, the meat can be eaten jerky-style or added to a variety of recipes. Once removed from the bone, it freezes well in vacuum-sealed packaging. In addition, any whole birds can be smoked using the jerky brines in this section. Turkey, duck and goose brines are interchangeable.

Turkey makes very good jerky and is a great way to eat larger, older toms. Ducks and geese are also great candidates for jerky as their meat is firm, more like beef than poultry.

Steps To Making Jerky

1. THE CUT

Most importantly, you want to start with a clean product. Take time to trim all visible fat, blood vessels and bloodshot spots from the meat as it can prevent proper drying and turn rancid in storage. Also, cut out any tendons and gristle as these only get tougher upon dehydration.

When dealing with large geese, swans, sandhill cranes and turkey, there are two ways to cut meat for jerky, cutting "with" or "against" the grain. Cutting against or cross-grain, makes an easy-to-bite piece of jerky. Cutting with the grain yields more traditional jerky strips and may need to be sliced for serving.

Turkey thigh meat can be cut with the grain into short strips and breast meat can be cut with or against the grain. Be sure not to cut turkey meat too thin. For jerky, it should be at least 1/4" thick. The breasts of smaller ducks are little and may

only yield one piece of jerky; they can also be butterflied into one large piece. Length doesn't matter, but when drying meat it helps to have uniform thickness. A rule of thumb with jerky is that the smallest piece should be slightly larger than your index finger. Uniform cuts will allow you to smoke multiple species of birds in the same batch.

2. THE BRINE

Salt and sugar are the two necessary ingredients for making jerky. Wet and dry brines both work well for game birds. Always prepare brine in non-corrosive bowls such as glass or stainless steel. Crocks work well for extra large batches but it is tough to find room in the refrigerator for these larger vessels. Prepare enough brine so all meat will be fully submerged. More brine is better than not enough.

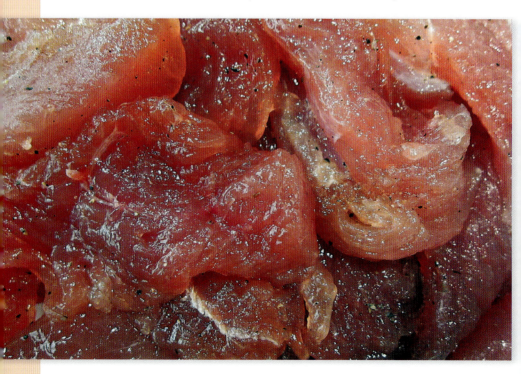

Whisk wet brine ingredients until sugar is dissolved. Once meat is added, stir to be sure brine has come into contact with all meat slices. Use a plate as a weight to keep meat fully submerged in the brine. Brine in the refrigerator or somewhere cool (under 50°). Never rinse brine off meat unless specified in the recipe.

3. ADDITIONAL SEASONINGS

Additional seasonings are optional. As soon as meat is placed on smoker racks and still damp, additional seasonings can be added. Avoid adding fresh herbs as they can yield a scorched flavor during the smoking process. Additions that work well are no-salt seasonings such as cajun, BBQ or lemon pepper. For sweet tasting jerky a light sprinkle of sugar or drizzle of honey adds a nice glaze to the finished product. Some seasonings, like apple juice, can be sprayed on for a sweet taste.

4. THE DRY

Jerky always smokes better if it is allowed to air-dry before going into the smoker. If too much liquid drips into the bottom of the smoker it can burn and taint the flavor. Place meat on to smoker racks and slightly elevate. If there is no worry of bugs or debris, this can be done outside or in a garage. It works well in the kitchen and the process is sped-up with the use of a counter top fan. If rushed for time, this step can be skipped but at least blot meat with paper towels to remove excessive moisture. The goal is to get a glaze forming on the meat so when it begins to cook in the smoker, flavors will be locked-in and it won't dry out too quickly.

To prevent off-flavors, clean smoker racks after each use (ours clean-up great in the dishwasher) and line the bottom of the smoker with a fresh layer of foil before each smoking session. This keeps the smoke clean and helps prevent corrosion of smoker parts.

5. THE SMOKE

When smoking, we like to burn chips for 1-3 hours to give a deep smoke flavor. For a smoker like the Little Chief, we go through 2 pans of chips. In a Bradley or Traeger, we have the pellets or bisquettes going for about 1/2 of the smoking time. A Camp Chef, propane-fed Smoke Vault only needs one large pan of chips.

The most important part of the smoking stage is to keep the smoker under 200°, preferably, between 150°-180°. As far as actual smoke time, *every brand of smoker works differently.* Follow the manufacturers instructions for the first few recipes and then start experimenting with what works best for you. Most smokers behave differently with the outside temperature, too. Take into consideration shorter smoke times in the summer and much longer times in the winter. Wind can also be a factor in smoking time.

When working with smaller smokers, we use an insulated cover which is worth the added cost. If possible, some smokers can be left in the box for added insulation. Make sure this doesn't present a fire hazard. *Never leave smokers unattended and always make sure they are in a well ventilated area on a fire-safe base like rock or concrete.* If using multiple smokers, pay close attention to electricity loads as some can easily throw breakers.

Jerky is done when it is dry but still flexible. It is difficult to get all jerky done at the same time due to the heat distribution of most smokers. When the first racks are done, one option is to bring it all inside and finish it in the oven at 165°. Set the timer for 15 minute intervals and take jerky out as it finishes. Another option is to leave it in the smoker, rotating pieces on the racks and moving them to the warmer spots in the smoker. Frequently check and remove pieces as they are done.

The longer jerky dries, the more preserved it becomes. Jerky that is so dry it will snap, does not need to be stored under refrigeration. Tiffany's grandpa's jerky always sits in a burlap sack at the side of his wood stove, all year—we never attempt to eat this jerky without a pocket knife to cut paper-thin slices with.

We prefer our jerky softer, therefore we keep our finished product refrigerated up to 2 weeks or frozen up to 1 year.

6. THE FINISH

The final step for jerky is an important one if you want to retain a softer, easier to chew, finished product. It must properly cool to retain moisture and deep smoke flavor. In a large glass bowl place warm pieces of jerky. Immediately cover with plastic wrap. Place in the refrigerator. As the jerky finishes–either outside in the smoker or inside in the oven–add it to the bowl, always covering it back up. Moisture will accumulate on the plastic. Every once in a while, flick that moisture back into the cooling jerky and lightly toss the bowl around, mixing up the jerky. When finished, package for storage.

7. PRESERVING/STORAGE

When jerky is done and completely cooled, keep refrigerated or immediately freeze. At this point, we vacuum seal jerky as it is slightly soft and the ends won't puncture the sealer bags. Use smaller bags with about a dozen pieces in it. Label and freeze immediately. Once unthawed, the jerky tastes like it just came out of the smoker. We've kept it up to a year in the freezer. If you get a lot of game meat, making it into jerky right away can save loads of freezer space. It's also wonderful to be able to grab a bag to go at a moment's notice.

Basic Jerky

Simply put, this is the base for jerky. This recipe allows you to use favorite flavors to create your own signature jerky. Keep salt in mind, as many commercial seasoning blends are 50% or more salt. If this is the case, reduce the amount of curing salt used. The best bet is to use salt-free seasonings, as they carry the most flavor.

- 3 pounds turkey, duck or goose, sliced for jerky
- 1 quart water
- 1/4 cup Morton's Tender Quick* or curing salt
- 1/4 cup white sugar
- 2-4 tablespoons salt-free seasoning blend
- 2 teaspoons liquid smoke (optional)

See Jerky Instructions, page 118.

Soy Molasses Jerky

- 3 pounds turkey, sliced for jerky
- 1 quart water
- 1/2 cup brown sugar
- 1/4 cup kosher salt
- 2 tablespoons molasses
- 2 tablespoons soy sauce
- 1 tablespoon granulated garlic
- 1 tablespoon granulated onion

See Jerky Instructions, page 118.

Pepper Jerky

- 3 pounds turkey, sliced for jerky
- 1 quart water
- 1/2 cup brown sugar
- 1/3 cup kosher salt
- 1 tablespoon black pepper
- 1 teaspoon cayenne pepper

See Jerky Instructions, page 118.

Honey-Orange Jerky

- 3 pounds turkey, duck or goose, sliced for jerky
- 3 cups water
- 1/2 cup orange juice
- 1/4 cup white sugar
- 1/4 cup honey
- 1/4 cup Morton's Tender Quick* or curing salt
- 1/2 tablespoon granulated onion
- 1/2 tablespoon garlic powder
- 1 teaspoon white pepper (optional)

See Jerky Instructions, page 118.

Teriyaki Jerky

- 2-3 pounds duck and/or goose, sliced for jerky
- 3 cups apple juice
- 1 cup teriyaki sauce
- 1/4 cup non-iodized salt
- 1/3 cup brown sugar
- 1 teaspoon garlic juice

See Jerky Instructions, page 118.

Five-Spice Jerky

- 3 pounds turkey, sliced for jerky
- 1 quart water
- 1/4 cup honey
- 1/4 cup soy sauce
- 2 tablespoons Morton's Tender Quick* or curing salt
- 1 tablespoon Chinese 5-Spice
- 1 tablespoon granulated garlic
- 1/2 tablespoon white pepper

See Jerky Instructions, page 118.

Herbed Jerky

- 2-3 pounds duck and/or goose, sliced for jerky
- 1 quart water
- 1/4 cup non-iodized salt
- 1/2 cup white sugar
- 2 cups fresh parsley, chopped
- 1 cup fresh cilantro, chopped
- 5-6 sprigs rosemary, chopped
- 2 tablespoons coriander seeds, crushed
- 1 tablespoon dried oregano
- 1 teaspoon white pepper, ground

See Jerky Instructions, page 118.

Red Hickory Jerky

- 2-3 pounds duck and/or goose, sliced for jerky
- 2 cups red wine
- 2 cups water
- 1/4 cup Morton's Tender Quick* or curing salt
- 2 tablespoons granulated garlic
- 2 tablespoons granulated onion
- 2 tablespoons cracked black pepper
- 1 tablespoon liquid smoke, hickory flavor

See Jerky Instructions, at right.

Savory Garlic Jerky

- 2-3 pounds goose breasts, sliced for jerky
- 1 quart water
- 1/3 cup Morton's Tender Quick* or curing salt
- 1 tablespoon brown sugar
- 4 cloves fresh garlic, minced
- 2 teaspoons granulated garlic or garlic powder
- 1 teaspoon black or white pepper
- 2 teaspoons liquid smoke

See Jerky Instructions, at right.

*Morton's Tender Quick is a product we have used for many years. It helps flavors fully absorb into the meat and helps keep meat from excessively drying-out during the smoking process. Morton's Tender Quick is a combination of salt and other curing ingredients. Morton's Sugar Cure can be used in place of Morton's Tender Quick. Kosher salt, canning and pickling salt or curing salt can be substituted in equal parts for Morton's Tender Quick. Other quick cures on the market are Speed Cure, Insta-cure, Prague Powder and pink curing salt. Experiment with these products to find the ratio that appeals to you.

JERKY INSTRUCTIONS:

When slicing meat for jerky, the traditional cut is in strips that go with the grain. In a large ceramic or glass bowl, mix all brine ingredients with a wire whisk until ingredients are dissolved. Add meat, mix thoroughly, and put a plate on top to be sure all meat remains submerged. Soak 8-10 hours, refrigerated, stirring occasionally.

Drain brine and remove meat. Do not rinse meat. If additional flavor is desired, sprinkle pepper or other seasonings (salt-free only) on meat at this time.

Place on racks and let air-dry for up to 1 hour or pat dry. Follow smoking directions on your smoker. Cooking times vary greatly and depend on make and model of smoker and outside weather conditions. Keep the temperature of the smoker between 150° and 200°.

Check for doneness after 3 hours. Larger cuts of jerky can be finished on a baking sheet in the oven at 165°, check every 15 minutes.

When jerky is done, place in a glass bowl and cover with plastic wrap under refrigeration until cool. Keep refrigerated or freeze (vacuum sealing works best) if storing for an extended period of time.

DRY BRINING

Here's another option for making jerky. Rather than soaking meat in water or other liquids, dry brining is the process of combining key ingredients to infuse flavor and begin the curing process. In any dry brine, sugar and salt are the primary ingredients. Other ingredients depend on personal choice and what flavors you desire. The options for dry brining flavors are limitless.

Basic Dry Brine

- 4-5 pounds meat, sliced for jerky
- 1/2 cup brown sugar
- 1/4 cup Morton's Tender Quick* or 1/4 cup kosher salt
- 1 tablespoon black pepper
- Additional seasonings as desired (i.e. cayenne pepper, lemon pepper, smoked paprika, cumin or any salt-free seasoning)
- 2 teaspoons liquid smoke (optional)

In a large ceramic or glass bowl, mix all brine ingredients with a wire whisk until ingredients are thoroughly combined. Add meat to dry brine, mix thoroughly with hands, massaging cure into the meat. Add liquid smoke at this time, if desired. Cover bowl with a plate or plastic wrap. Soak 8-10 hours, refrigerated, stirring/massaging occasionally.

Drain brine, if it has accumulated, and remove meat. Do not rinse meat. Place on racks and let air dry for up to 1 hour or pat dry. Follow smoking directions on your smoker. Cooking times vary greatly and depend on make and model of smoker and outside weather conditions. Keep the temperature of the smoker between 150° and 200°.

Check for doneness after 3 hours. Larger cuts of jerky can be finished on a baking sheet in the oven at 165°, check every 15 minutes.

When jerky is done, place in a glass bowl and cover with plastic wrap under refrigeration until cool. Keep refrigerated or freeze (vacuum sealing works best) if storing for an extended period of time.

Sauces, Rubs, Marinades & More

SAUCES

Chili-Apricot Sauce

- 1/2 cup apricot jam
- 3 tablespoons apple cider vinegar
- 1/2 teaspoon chili powder
- 1/2 teaspoon red pepper flakes
- 1/2 teaspoon salt

In a small saucepan, bring all ingredients to a boil on medium-high heat. Turn heat to low and simmer until ready to serve.

Five-Spice BBQ Sauce

- 1/3 cup hoisin sauce
- 2 tablespoons honey
- 1 tablespoon rice vinegar
- 1 tablespoon sesame oil
- 1 clove garlic, pureed
- 1 teaspoon five-spice powder
- 1/4 teaspoon black pepper

In a small saucepan, bring all ingredients to a boil on medium-high heat. Turn heat to low and simmer until ready to serve.

Green Sauce

- 1 cup fresh cilantro leaves
- Juice from 2 lemons
- 2 tablespoons sugar
- 2 cloves garlic
- 2 large jalapeno peppers, seeded and chopped
- 1/4 cup walnut pieces
- 1/2 teaspoon salt

In a food processor or mini-chopper, blend all ingredients until thoroughly combined. Serve immediately or keep refrigerated in a sealed container. This sauce pairs with game bird meat or can be used for a tortilla chip dip.

Honey BBQ Sauce

- 1 green bell pepper, chopped
- 1 onion, chopped
- 3 cloves garlic, crushed
- 1/2 cup chili sauce
- 1/2 cup ketchup
- 1/2 cup honey
- 1/4 cup Worcestershire sauce
- 2 tablespoons apple cider vinegar
- 1 tablespoon mustard
- 1 teaspoon paprika

In a large saucepan, bring all ingredients to a boil on medium-high heat. Turn heat to low and simmer 25-30 minutes. Remove onion and pepper chunks before serving if desired.

Marinara Sauce

- 2 tablespoons olive oil
- 1/2 onion, finely chopped
- 3 cloves garlic, pureed
- 1 cup diced tomatoes
- 3 tablespoons tomato paste
- 1/3 cup red wine
- 1/2 teaspoon Italian seasoning
- 1/4 cup parsley, chopped
- 8-10 fresh basil leaves, chopped
  red pepper flakes (optional)
- Salt and pepper to taste

In a large skillet, heat olive oil on medium-high heat. Sauté onion and garlic 2-3 minutes. Add remaining ingredients except for fresh basil. Bring sauce to a boil and reduce heat to low. Salt and pepper to taste. Simmer at least 15 minutes. Add basil during the last few minutes of cooking time.

Mole Sauce

- 1 tablespoon olive oil
- 1 cup onion, diced
- 3 cloves garlic, diced
- 1 tablespoon cocoa powder
- 1 1/2 teaspoons cumin
- 1 teaspoon cinnamon
- 1/2 teaspoon salt
- 1/4 teaspoon black pepper
- 1 6-ounce can tomato paste
- 1 4-ounce can diced green chilies
- 1 cup water
- 2 tablespoons fresh cilantro, chopped (optional)

In a medium skillet, heat olive oil on medium-high heat. Saute onion and garlic until tender. Continue sauteing all spices and tomato paste until fragrant, 3-5 minutes. Add chilies and water. Simmer 5-10 minutes on low heat. Spoon sauce over cooked game birds or use as a sauce for slow cooking. Garnish with fresh cilantro if desired.

Mushroom Sauce

- 1 tablespoon olive oil
- 2 cups mushrooms, chopped
- 2 tablespoons onion, diced
- 1 tablespoon flour
- 1 teaspoon fresh thyme or 1/2 teaspoon dried
- 1/2 cup dry sherry or red wine
- 1/2 cup turkey stock or chicken broth
- 3 tablespoons sour cream or whipped cream
- 2 tablespoons fresh parsley, chopped

In a medium skillet, heat olive oil on medium-high heat. Saute mushroom and onion until tender. Sprinkle flour over mushrooms and saute 1-2 minutes. Add thyme, sherry and broth and bring to a boil until slightly thickened. Turn heat to low, add cream and parsley. Simmer until warm throughout. Spoon sauce over cooked game birds or use as a sauce for slow cooking.

Orange Nut Sauce

- 1 tablespoon olive oil
- 1/3 cup pine nuts or slivered almonds
- 1/4 cup green onion, chopped
- 1 tablespoon parsley, chopped
- 1 teaspoon orange zest
- 1/2 cup turkey stock or chicken broth
- 1/2 cup orange juice
- 2 teaspoons cornstarch
- 1 tablespoon water

In a small skillet, heat olive oil on medium-high heat. Toast nuts 2-3 minutes or until browned. Add remaining ingredients except for cornstarch and water. In a small bowl mix cornstarch and water until smooth. Add cornstarch mixture to sauce. Bring to a boil, stir until thickened. Remove from heat and serve immediately.

Peanut Sauce

- 1/2 cup creamy peanut butter
- 1/2 cup coconut milk
- 1 tablespoon lime juice
- 2 teaspoons fish sauce
- 2 teaspoons soy sauce
- 1 teaspoon sesame oil
- 1/2-1 teaspoon chili paste
- 1/2 teaspoon curry powder

In a medium bowl, whisk all ingredients until fully combined. Use for a dipping sauce for satay or use as a sauce for slow-cooking game birds.

Raspberry Sauce

- 1 cup raspberry jam
- 3 tablespoons white wine vinegar
- 2 tablespoons orange juice
- 1 tablespoon orange zest
- Salt to taste

Combine raspberry jam, orange juice, and vinegar. Bring to a boil. Boil 2-3 minutes, until sauce is reduced and slightly thickened. Remove from heat, add orange zest and salt to taste.

Soy Dipping Sauce

- 1/3 cup soy sauce
- 2 tablespoons green onion or chives, finely chopped
- 2 tablespoons rice or white vinegar
- 1 teaspoon sugar
- 2-3 Thai hot peppers or 1-2 habanero, minced

In a small bowl, mix all ingredients until thoroughly combined. This sauce can also be used for a marinade or sauce over meat, seafood or rice.

Teriyaki Sauce

- 1 cup water
- 1 tablespoon cornstarch
- 1/4 cup soy sauce
- 1/4 cup brown sugar
- 1 teaspoon powdered ginger
- 1 teaspoon granulated garlic

In a small bowl, mix cornstarch with water. In a small saucepan, mix remaining ingredients and bring to a boil on high heat until sugar dissolves. Slowly add cornstarch/water mixture and stir until thickened, 1-2 minutes. Remove from heat and use immediately or cool and refrigerate.

RUBS

Cajun Rub

- 1 tablespoon smoked paprika
- 2 teaspoons garlic powder
- 2 teaspoons onion powder
- 1 teaspoon oregano
- 1 teaspoon thyme
- 1 teaspoon black pepper
- 1 teaspoon white pepper
- 1/2 teaspoon cayenne pepper

In a small bowl or sealable plastic bag, mix all ingredients until thoroughly combined.

Coffee Rub

- 3 tablespoons coffee, finely ground
- 1 tablespoon salt
- 1 tablespoon brown sugar
- 1 teaspoon smoked paprika
- 1 teaspoon granulated garlic
- 1 teaspoon unsweetened cocoa powder
- 1 teaspoon black pepper

In a small bowl or sealable plastic bag, mix all ingredients until thoroughly combined.

Jerk Rub

- 1 tablespoon dried minced onion
- 2 teaspoons dried thyme
- 1 teaspoon black pepper
- 1 teaspoon ground allspice
- 1/2 teaspoon salt
- 1/2 teaspoon granulated garlic
- 1/2 teaspoon ground cinnamon
- 1/4 teaspoon cayenne pepper

In a small bowl or sealable plastic bag, mix all ingredients until thoroughly combined.

Moroccan Rub

- 1/4 cup sugar
- 1 tablespoon salt
- 2 teaspoons whole coriander seeds
- 2 teaspoons whole cumin seeds
- 1 teaspoon black peppercorns

Crush everything with a spice grinder or mortar and pestle until thoroughly combined.

MARINADES

Asian Marinade

- 1/3 cup dry sherry
- 1/4 cup soy sauce
- 1/4 cup oyster sauce
- 2 tablespoons honey
- 1 teaspoon ground ginger
- 1 teaspoon dry mustard
- 2 cloves garlic, minced

In a medium bowl or sealable plastic bag, mix all ingredients until thoroughly combined.

Greek Marinade

- 2 tablespoons olive oil
- 1 lemon, juice of
- 4 cloves garlic, crushed
- 1 teaspoon dried oregano
- 1 teaspoon salt
- 1 teaspoon freshly ground black pepper
- 1 large red onion, cut into 1" chunks

In a medium bowl or sealable plastic bag, mix all ingredients until thoroughly combined.

Indonesian Marinade

- 1/4 cup shallots, chopped
- 2 cloves garlic, minced
- 1-2 red chili peppers, diced
- 2 tablespoons fresh ginger, minced
- 2 tablespoons olive oil
- 1 tablespoon coriander
- 1 tablespoon dark brown sugar
- 1 tablespoon soy sauce

In a medium bowl or sealable plastic bag, mix all ingredients until thoroughly combined.

Japanese Marinade

- 3 green onions, chopped
- 1/4 cup soy sauce
- 1/4 cup mirin
- 2 tablespoons sake
- 1 tablespoon sugar

In a medium bowl or sealable plastic bag, mix all ingredients until thoroughly combined.

Lemon Ginger Marinade

- 1/4 cup lemon juice
- 1/4 cup teriyaki or Worcestershire sauce
- 2 tablespoons honey
- 3"-5" fresh ginger root, sliced

In a medium bowl or sealable plastic bag, mix all ingredients until thoroughly combined.

Orange Marinade

- 1/2 cup orange juice
- 2 tablespoons soy sauce
- 2 tablespoons white wine vinegar
- 2 tablespoons hoisin sauce
- 1 teaspoon garlic powder
- 1 teaspoon orange zest

In a medium bowl or sealable plastic bag, mix all ingredients until thoroughly combined.

Teriyaki Marinade

- 1/4 cup soy
- 1/4 cup cream sherry
- 1/4 cup olive oil
- 3 tablespoons shallot, diced
- 1" ginger root, peeled & grated
- 1 tablespoon brown sugar

In a medium bowl or sealable plastic bag, mix all ingredients until thoroughly combined. For Teriyaki Sauce: Reduce olive oil to 1 tablespoon. In a small saucepan, saute shallot and ginger in olive oil on medium-high heat.

MORE
Mandarin Pancakes

- 1 cup flour
- 1/3 cup boiling water
- 1 tablespoon sesame oil

In a medium bowl, mix pancake ingredients until dough forms into a ball. Knead until dough is smooth, about 5 minutes. Roll dough into a ball and cover with plastic wrap. Let dough rest 30 minutes at room temperature.

Roll dough into a log shape. Cut dough into equal sizes: 10 pieces = large, 8" pancakes, 20 pieces = small, 4" pancakes.

On a lightly floured surface, roll pieces as thin as possible with a rolling pin. Heat a non-stick pan or griddle on medium-high heat. Cook pancakes until they just begin to brown (about 1 minute), flip and cook on the other side. Keep covered until ready to serve. Serve warm or at room temperature with Peking Duck.

Pupusas

- 2 cups masa harina
- 1 cup warm water

- Oil or butter for cooking

In a medium bowl, mix masa harina with water until dough forms into a ball. Add more water if necessary to make a moist, yet firm dough. Roll dough into a ball and cover with plastic wrap. Let dough rest 15 minutes at room temperature.

Roll dough into a log shape. Cut 10-12 even slices. Press dough as flat as possible using the palms of your hand, a tortilla press or a rolling pin (sandwich dough between wax paper so it won't stick).

Heat a non-stick pan or griddle on medium-high heat. Lightly grease pan with oil or butter. Cook pupusas until they just begin to brown (about 1 minute), flip and cook on the other side. Keep covered until ready to serve. Serve warm or at room temperature with fajitas or chili.

Cran-Cherry Pecan Chutney

- 1 cup sugar
- 1 cup water
- 1/2 cup red wine
- 1/2 cup dried cherries
- 1 1/2 cups fresh cranberries
- 2/3 cup pecans, finely chopped
- Zest of 1/2 lemon
- 1/2 teaspoon cinnamon

In a medium saucepan, bring all ingredients to a boil. Reduce heat and simmer 10-20 minutes. Serve warm or cool and refrigerate.

Cranberry Jalapeno Salsa

- 3 cups fresh or frozen cranberries
- 2 jalapeno peppers, seeded & chopped
- 1/2 cup cilantro, chopped
- 1" (1 tablespoon) fresh ginger, grated
- 1/2 cup sugar
- 1/2 teaspoon salt
- Juice & zest from 2 limes

Finely chop cranberries in a food chopper or processor. Place cranberries in a medium bowl. Finely chop peppers, cilantro and ginger until blended. Add to cranberries. Add remaining ingredients and mix until thoroughly combined. Refrigerate 30 minutes before serving.

Mango Salsa

- 2 cups mango, cubed
- 1 red bell pepper, finely chopped
- 2 green onions, chopped
- 1/4 cup cilantro leaves, chopped
- Juice of 1 lime
- 1 tablespoon ginger, minced
- 1 tablespoon brown sugar
- 1 tablespoon fish sauce (optional)
- 2-3 teaspoons hot sauce or chili sauce

In a medium bowl, gently toss all ingredients until combined. Let sit, refrigerated, at least 30 minutes before serving.

Fresh Salsa

- 6 Roma-style tomatoes, chopped
- 1/2 cup bell pepper, chopped
- 1/2 cup onion, diced
- 2 jalapeno peppers, diced
- 2 tablespoons lemon or lime juice
- 1 teaspoon sugar
- 1/2 teaspoon salt
- 1/2 teaspoon cumin
- 1/2 teaspoon chili powder
- Black pepper to taste
- Hot pepper sauce to taste (optional)

In a medium bowl, gently toss all ingredients until combined.

Rhubarb Salsa

- 2 cups rhubarb, finely chopped
- 1/2 cup bell pepper, finely chopped
- 1/3 cup red onion, finely chopped
- 1/4 cup cilantro, chopped
- 1 4-ounce can green chilies
- 2 tablespoons lime juice
- 1 tablespoon brown sugar
- 1/4-1/2 teaspoon cumin
- Salt and pepper to taste

Submerge chopped rhubarb in boiling water 2 minutes. Drain well and cool. In a medium bowl, gently toss all remaining ingredients and rhubarb until combined.

Sauerkraut Relish

- 4 cups sauerkraut, drained
- 1 cup celery, diced
- 2/3 cup green pepper or jalapeno, diced
- 1/2 cup red onion, diced
- 1 4-ounce jar diced pimento
- 1/4 cup sugar
- 1/2 teaspoon celery seed
- Salt and pepper to taste

In a large bowl, mix all ingredients until sugar is dissolved. Marinate, refrigerated, at least 2 hours for optimal flavor.

Indian Paste

- 1 teaspoon cumin
- 1 teaspoon dry mustard
- 1 teaspoon ginger
- 1 teaspoon turmeric
- 1/2 teaspoon black pepper
- 1/2 teaspoon cayenne pepper
- 1/2 teaspoon cinnamon
- 1/2 teaspoon coriander
- 3 cloves garlic, pureed
- 1/3 cup white wine vinegar
- 2 tablespoons tomato paste
- 1 tablespoon vegetable oil

In a small bowl, mix all ingredients until thoroughly combined.

Basil Pesto

- 1 1/2 cups basil leaves
- 1/2 cup parmesan cheese, grated
- 1/4 cup extra virgin olive oil
- 1/4 cup toasted pine nuts
- 2-4 cloves garlic
- Salt and pepper to taste.

Finely chop basil in a food chopper or processor. Add remaining ingredients and blend until smooth.

Sundried Tomato Pesto

- 1 4-ounce jar or 1/2 cup sundried tomatoes, packed in oil
- 1/3 cup fresh parsley leaves
- 1/4 cup fresh basil leaves
- 1/2 cup parmesan cheese, grated
- 1/2 cup walnuts
- 2 cloves garlic
- 2 tablespoons olive oil
- Salt and pepper to taste

Finely chop tomatoes, parsley and basil in a food chopper or processor. Add remaining ingredients and blend until smooth.

Herb Brine

- 3 cups water
- 1/3 cup brown sugar
- 2 tablespoons sea salt
- 1 tablespoon black pepper
- 8-10 fresh sage leaves or 4-5 dried
- 4 sprigs fresh thyme or 1 tablespoon dried
- 2 sprigs fresh rosemary or 1/2 tablespoon dried

If using fresh herbs; tear, chop or bruise, before adding to bring mixture. In a large bowl, mix brine ingredients until dissolved.

White Gravy

- 3 cups milk
- 3 tablespoons butter
- 3 tablespoons flour
- 1/2 teaspoon salt
- 1/4 teaspoon white pepper

In a large skillet, melt butter on medium-high heat. Add flour and whisk constantly, 1-2 minutes. Slowly add milk, whisking constantly until all milk is added and mixture comes to a low boil. Add salt and pepper, remove from heat and serve immediately.

Turkey Gravy

- 3 cups turkey/chicken stock or broth
- 3 tablespoons olive oil or butter
- 3 tablespoons flour
- 1/4 teaspoon white pepper

In a large skillet, melt butter or heat oil on medium-high heat. Add flour and whisk constantly, 1-2 minutes. Slowly add broth, whisking constantly until all broth is added and mixture comes to a low boil. Add pepper, remove from heat and serve immediately.

Appendix A: General Information

GENERAL HUNTING SEASONS

Generally speaking, bird hunting seasons throughout North America run pretty consistent from year to year, region to region. An exception would be the growing number of bird preserves that have helped produce more shooting opportunities and lengthened seasons in many states. In some states, preserve hunting for pheasant, chukar an quail runs from August well into the spring months.

For most wingshooters the fall season kicks-off with upland birds, usually in the form of dove or pigeon. There are many bird hunters across the country who share similar stories of their first bird hunting experience being for doves.

On the heels of dove and pigeon season comes more upland bird opportunities, these for quail and grouse. Often there's a generous overlapping of seasons where grouse and quail coexist, making for great shooting action and yielding some of the best eating meat in the woods.

Pheasant, partridge and waterfowl ring in the coming of fall with their openings. In some areas across the country, early waterfowling opportunities exist for both ducks and geese. These early hunts are usually in place to help manage overpopulated ducks and geese. Because these early hunts are largely for resident, non-migratory birds, they can be some of the best eating waterfowl around.

As the fall months progress, turkey, snipe and woodcock hunters take to the woods in search of not only some unique hunting action, but for tasty game. To the north, ptarmigan hunters also put their shooting skills to the test in the fall and winter months. In special draw regions, swan hunters take to the field in the fall, as do sandhill crane enthusiasts in the limited areas where these great-eating birds thrive.

In some flyways, late goose seasons are in place that extend well into spring. The purpose of these seasons is to keep birds—most commonly, snow geese—from growing too overpopulated to the point where they exceed the carrying capacity of their northerly nesting grounds. Such instances have occurred, leading to death by starvation and disease.

Wherever you live or plan to hunt, check that state's bird hunting regulations to gain insight as to what hunting seasons are open and when. Many bird hunters plan their trips to maximize hunting opportunities, that is, hit as many states as they can for as many species of birds as they can. It's a good plan, and a great testimony to the wonderful bird hunting we are so fortunate to have in North America.

HUNTABLE GAME BIRDS IN NORTH AMERICA

Upland Birds
Turkey
Blue Grouse
Ruffed Grouse
Sage Grouse
Sharptail Grouse
Spruce Grouse
Greater Prairie Chicken
Lesser Prairie Chicken
Willow Ptarmigan
Rock Ptarmigan
White Tailed Ptarmigan
California (Valley) Quail
Mountain Quail
Gambel's Quail
Scaled Quail
Bobwhite Quail
Mearns (Harlequin) Quail
Ringneck Pheasant
Chukar Partridge
Hungarian (Gray) Partridge
Mourning Dove
Band Tailed Pigeon
Snipe
Woodcock

Waterfowl
(Small Puddle Ducks)
Green-Winged Teal
Blue-Winged Teal
Cinnamon Teal

Medium Puddle Ducks
American Widgeon
Eurasian Widgeon
Wood Duck

Large Puddle Ducks
Mallard
Northern Pintail
Gadwall
Black Duck
Northern Shoveler

Diving Ducks
Greater Scaup
Lesser Scaup
Common Goldeneye
Barrow's Goldeneye
Redhead
Canvasback
Common Merganser
Hooded Merganser
Red-Breasted Merganser
Bufflehead
Ruddy Duck

Sea Ducks–
(some often found with
diving ducks)
Harlequin Duck
Long-Tailed Duck
    (Oldsquaw)
King Eider
Common Eider
Stellar's Eider
Spectacled Eider
Surf Scoter
Black Scoter
White-Winged Scoter

Geese, Swans & Cranes
Canada Goose
    (multiple subspecies)
Snow Goose (greater, lesser)
Blue Goose
Ross' Goose
White-Fronted Goose
Brant (Pacific, Atlantic)
Tundra Swan
Sandhill Crane

*Note: Some species were intentionally not included in these lists based on the fact they are infrequent visitor to North American flyways, are feral species, or their current populations don't allow for a legal hunting season at the time of this writing.

Appendix B:
Field Care, Plucking, Skinning

FIELD CARE

The best birds can be destroyed by inadequate handling in the field. Improper bleeding, delay or carelessness in gutting and failure to quickly cool meat can all make a major difference in the flavor of the end product. By following a few simple guidelines, the quality of the meat will come through in the final preparation. Think of how much work went into the hunt and give game birds the deluxe treatment they deserve.

Do not use a vest or bag to store birds while in the field, as this retains too much of their body heat. Instead, use a game strap to carry your birds afield. Once birds are taken, be sure to keep them cool and dry. Also, never pile up birds or put them in a closed container or hot vehicle (trunk or empty cooler), as the birds will literally cook in their own body heat, spoiling meat quickly.

Due to their light bone structure and thin intestinal walls, birds need to be bled and gutted as quickly as possible after being shot. Allowing air to circulate in the body cavity will greatly increase the quality of meat. Birds don't have much fat so their body heat is held in their internal organs (unlike big game that holds much of their body heat in muscle tissues), which explains why quickly cleaning them is so important.

If you're collecting several birds over the course of a day's hunt, it's wise to gut the birds as you shoot them. Keep a bottle of water handy, or rely on a stream, to rinse the body cavity and wash your hands, then continue hunting. Doing this will eliminate a surprising amount of the "gamey" taste birds often get blamed for, when really, it's the mishandling by hunters which is to blame.

For birds that are gut shot, the best advice is to immediately remove the internal organs. Bird meat can easily be tainted by a gut shot wound, and a quick inspection after the shot usually leaves no question as to the point of impact. Once the internal organs are removed, give the body cavity a thorough rinsing and let air-cool. One gut shot bird can ruin an entire dish, so be sure to clean every piece of meat.

Because birds are so fragile compared to big game, it's a good idea to cook them quickly after being taken or age them appropriately (See Appendix C). Make every effort possible to keep them cold until ready to cook, or freeze.

HOW TO BLEED A BIRD

Many wingshooters opt for bleeding their birds rather than field dressing them. Bleeding a bird is simply done by cutting the throat and letting the heads hang downward until bleeding stops. If you have to finish-off a crippled bird, ring it's neck first (breaking the neck), then bleed it out. Be sure the head stays attached to the carcass, as some states require this for legal transportation of harvested birds (check state regulations for details).

Bleeding a bird will optimize it's overall flavor. If you don't want to mess with blood potentially getting everywhere, gutting a bird will have the same effect as bleeding it. Be sure to remove all internal organs, including heart, liver and lungs, in order for proper bleeding to occur.

Note: If wanting to eat the gizzard, heart and/or liver, get them on ice or refrigerated as soon as possible. These organs should be consumed immediately as they don't require any aging.

HOW TO GUT A BIRD

Gutting a bird is easy, and is best done when they are still warm. Not only will gutting warm birds make organ removal easier, it allows the bird to completely bleed out and cool down, which will yield a much better tasting meat.

With a small knife, begin by making a shallow incision from the vent (anus) straight up to the edge of the breast bone. In densely feathered birds like waterfowl, it may be easier to make the initial incision from the breast, down toward the vent, cutting with the direction the feathers are laying. There's no need to pluck the bird first, especially when in the field.

Next, reach inside the body cavity, grab a handful of internal organs and gently pull them out. A gentle approach is best to prevent puncturing the thin intestinal walls. With small birds like doves, quail and teal, you may only be able to get a pair of fingers into the body cavity.

Be sure to remove all internal organs (stomach, intestines, gizzard, liver, heart, lungs and windpipe), completely. Note that the lungs of all birds lay tight against their back, by the back portion of the rib cage. It's crucial to remove every piece of lung, for these organs quickly rot and can taint the taste of your birds.

If your fingers are too large to pull out the lungs, use the tip of your knife to lift under the subcutaneous sheath that holds the lungs in place. From there, either continue peeling the lungs away from the ribs and spine with the knife, or your fingers. Once the lungs are free from both sides of the rib cage, all the way to the spine, they can be extracted in one piece. Should remnants of lung remain wedged between the ribs, use the tip of the knife blade to pick them free.

Be sure the trachea and esophagus are also removed. On small birds, they often come out with the initial extraction of the internal organs. For medium size birds the removal of the trachea and esophagus will likely have to be done independently of the internal organs. On large birds like turkey and geese, you'll likely need to wrap the trachea and esophagus around your fingers or hand and give a firm yank. Removing the trachea and esophagus not only ensures proper, thorough bleeding, it allows air to more freely move throughout the entire body cavity, cooling the meat.

When finished gutting the bird, rinse the body cavity and allow air to reach it so it can begin cooling. Once you get it down, it only takes a matter of seconds to gut a bird–it's that easy.

At this stage, birds can be aged with the feathers on, 2-4 days under refrigeration, or see chart on page 139 for species specific guidelines.

HOW TO PLUCK A BIRD

Plucking a bird sounds easy, and it can be, with the right birds. As a rule of thumb, most upland birds are easy to dry pluck (without first soaking them in water). The feathers of doves, pigeons, quail and grouse come out so easily, it's a wonder the feathers don't fly off their bodies in a heavy wind. Turkeys are the exception to the easy plucking of upland birds, which is why most people wet pluck or skin them.

Plucking waterfowl is a different story. Small ducks are fairly easy to pluck, but it gets more challenging as you progress to larger sized puddle ducks, diving ducks, sea ducks, then geese. This is because waterfowl spend a large part of their life on water, and rely on densely packed feathers, thick down and a thick, fatty skin to keep them warm.

Why pluck birds, not just skin them? Because game birds have so little fat in their muscles, when cooked they become dry and gamey tasting. Cooking birds with the skin on helps retain moisture and flavor.

When plucking birds, be careful not to grab handfuls of feathers and start yanking, as this could rip the skin. Once a bird skin rips, it's challenging to finish plucking it with the skin intact.

To pluck a bird, grab it by the neck or head with one hand, grab a few feathers with fingers of the other hand and start pulling in a downward motion, toward the tail. Pulling with the quills allows the feathers to easily slip out of the follicle in the skin and also helps prevent the skin from ripping.

Work around the bird ensuring all feathers are removed. If plucking birds in the field and transporting them in a vehicle, be aware that many states require one full wing to stay attached to the body (along with the head), for species and sex identification purposes. If plucking birds at home, it is easier to do so with the wings removed.

Remove the wings of birds by either cutting at the wrist joint (where the radius and ulna meet) or breaking along the wing shaft. Remember, bird bones are hollow and the bones of the wings, in particular, are very strong. If wings are broken, either intentionally or upon being shot or making impact with the ground, be sure all sharp fragments are removed before cooking or serving.

It's a good idea to keep the feet attached to a bird while plucking, as this provides something to hold on to as you rotate and move the carcass around for thorough plucking. With all the feathers removed, you'll see small, downy feathers still intact. These are so small they are nearly impossible to pluck, but should be removed.

Rather than spending time plucking these tiny, fine feathers, try singeing them with a torch. A quick pass with a flame will burn the feathers, giving you a clean, fully plucked bird. Rarely do we eat the skin of a game bird so if there are a few feathers or a bit of stubble, it comes off with the skin, prior to eating.

Plucking an obviously body shot bird should be avoided, as cooking it whole will result in an unpleasant, gamey taste. Instead, skin these birds and cut out all bloodshot areas, making sure to remove shotgun pellets from the meat. Typically, as a pellet enters the muscle, it takes with it downy feathers. This down often wraps

around the pellet, covering it up. The down feather may be easy to see lodged inside the muscle, but the pellet may not. Be sure to remove all feathers imbedded in the meat, as there's a good chance a pellet is in there, too. For body shot birds, cut the meat into strips, cleaning all bloodshot areas and use the pieces of meat for stir-fry, stews or freeze for later use.

Birds are easiest to pluck while still warm, but should only be plucked right away if they can be immediately refrigerated. Gutting birds in the field and leaving the feathers on is a good way to transport them, whereby protecting the meat from bruising and dirt. Plucking is most efficiently done back at camp or home.

If you're one who gets a lot of waterfowl over the course of the year, and prefers plucking your birds rather than skinning them, it might be worth investing in a mechanical plucker. There are numerous styles and types of mechanical bird pluckers out there, and people use them on all sorts of birds. Mostly, mechanical pluckers are used to strip the feathers from harder-to-pluck birds, like ducks and geese. These devices can save you hours of hand-plucking over the course of a season.

OTHER PLUCKING OPTIONS

Dry-plucking a bird can be challenging and time consuming, and there are a couple other options worth trying. One is wet-plucking, the other is dipping the bird in melted paraffin wax.

When wet-plucking a bird, bring a large pot of water to a boil. Be sure there is enough water to fully submerge the bird(s). This is best done outside. While the water is reaching a boil, remove the wings from the bird(s) and pluck out the tail feathers.

Once the water reaches a boil, grab the bird by the feet and completely submerge it. Grab the feet rather than the head, as once rigor mortis sets in, they provide better leverage to submerge the carcass. Hold the bird under water for seven seconds, no longer. Submerging it for too long will result in the meat starting to cook.

Remove the bird, then grab it by the head (wearing thick rubber gloves helps, as the head is hot) and start plucking. Pull the feathers in a downward motion, toward the tail, as pulling against the way they grow will tear the skin. Having a trash bag nearby, to drop the plucked feathers into, helps quickly move the process along.

Wet-plucking works best on upland birds, especially turkeys that can take a long time to dry-pluck. Wet-plucking waterfowl can be a challenge, however, since their feathers are so dense and so hydrophobic. For waterfowl, try plucking them by using wax.

There are two types of wax that can be used in plucking waterfowl, paraffin wax and duck wax. Paraffin wax, like that used in candle making and home canning, can be purchased online or from supply companies. Duck wax is what serious waterfowlers prefer, as it sticks to the feathers in larger, easier to peel pieces than the paraffin. Duck wax can be purchased online or in select sporting goods stores in five or 10-pound lots.

Outside, heat a pot of water to about 160°F. Do not bring the water to a boil and do not get the water too hot or it will not allow the wax to evenly buildup on the surface. As the water heats up, add your wax, allowing it to melt and rise to the surface. When the wax melts, it should be 1/4- to 1/2-inch thick on the surface. If it's not thick enough, either cool the water or add more wax. A good rule of thumb ratio is 25% wax and 75% water.

Prior to waxing your bird, remove the wings close to the bird's body, then dry-pluck the tail feathers and other large body feathers. Holding the bird by the feet (or head), dip and gently move it around in the melted wax. The objective is to allow about 1/2-inch or so of wax to buildup on the bird. Once evenly covered in wax, remove and let cool until the wax is hardened, usually about 10 minutes.

Once hardened, peel the wax in a downward motion, toward the tail-end. Wax and feathers will come off, together. When done peeling you can put the wax back in the hot water and allow to re-melt. Skim feathers off the top and re-dip the carcass as needed. Repeat dipping, cooling and peeling process until all feathers and down are removed.

When finished, the wax can be re-melted and feathers skimmed off the top. Let the water cool and the wax harden, storing it for future use.

HOW TO SKIN A BIRD

If not plucking a bird, skinning it is another option. This is a great option when there isn't time for plucking. There are numerous cooking methods throughout the book for skinned birds. Skinned birds can be used whole or they can be breasted-out. If breasting-out a bird, remove thighs and legs and cook separately. Many recipes suggest cooking breast meat separately from leg and thigh meat due to the differences in fat content and cooking time.

Birds should only be skinned if they can be immediately refrigerated or placed in a cold ice chest. Skinning is much faster than plucking, but because the protective skin has been removed, these birds cannot be aged under refrigeration for more than a day or two as they'll dry out.

To skin a bird, pick up where you left off when gutting it. For all upland birds, simply run a thumb beneath the skin and begin tearing it away from the breast bone. The thin skin of upland birds easily tears. Continue peeling the skin down the sides of each breast, all the way to the wings. If the wings haven't already been removed, now is a good time to sever them at the wrist joint.

Continue peeling the skin off the carcass, working your way around the back and tail section. Peel the skin down each leg, much like you'd unroll a sock, and sever each leg at the knee joint.

With the skin now loose from the legs, back and breast, work the skin around the shoulders, all the way to the neck. Sever the neck at desired point.

For birds like turkeys, geese and some ducks, it may be necessary to use a knife and make an incision through the skin from the base of the keel all the way to where the wishbone meets the sternum. Be careful not to slice too deeply, into the meat. Once an incision has been made, peel off the skin as described above.

If looking to breast-out your birds, that's simple and quick. Peel away the skin from both sides of the breast, as described above, all the way down to the base of the wings and the back of the rib cage. Next, take a sharp fillet knife and slice into the breast, keeping the blade firmly running against the keel as you cut. Continue filleting the meat away from the keel and breast bone until removed from the bone. Sever the chunk of breast meat where it attaches to the shoulder, at the base of the wing, and repeat on the other side.

Be sure and remove the legs and thighs of all game birds, as this is required by law. Simply peel away the skin from these parts, cut the foot off at the knee and remove the leg from the body by cutting through the ball-and-socket joint. Legs and thighs, separate of the breast, offer excellent eating options.

Appendix C: Aging Game Birds

Opinions on how best to age upland game birds and waterfowl run the gamut. There are those that adhere to the motto "fresh birds are the best birds" and others that wouldn't think of eating a bird before it had aged at least a week. Differences on aging temperatures and whether or not birds should be gutted prior to aging exist as well.

When we lived in the Alaskan Arctic, during the waterfowl migrations local hunters would pile their birds in unheated storage rooms and entryways immediately after the harvest, saving gutting and plucking until right before eating. Things changed when we lived on the equator, where nothing is allowed to age. Even the chickens we picked out at the open-air market were alive until we paid for them. In other words, where you hunt has a lot do with how you care for and age your birds.

We have had delicious birds, both fresh and aged, and find that it comes down to time and personal preference. Most of the time we have some type of wild game meat in our refrigerator at one aging stage or another. It is important to note that wild game can be aged right after it is killed or aged after it has been frozen. When aging game birds, follow the guidelines on the next page to attain the best eating meat.

AGING GUIDELINES

- Only head-shot birds should be aged without skinning.
- Skinned birds should not age more than 24 hours.
- Place birds on a rack, or hang by head or feet, for proper ventilation.
- Age meat uncovered.

- Juvenile birds need no aging time.
- Pen/planted/farm-raised birds don't need aging.
- If ducks smell fishy, do not age as gamey flavor will concentrate.
- Dry-pluck birds that have hung for longer than 3 days.

AGING TIME & BIRD SPECIES

The following aging times are suggested for head-shot birds that have been gutted and plucked.

Less than 24 hours aging time:
Juvenile birds
Pen/farm-raised birds
Quail
Snipe
Dove
Pigeon
Teal
Skinned birds

2-3 days aging time:
Grouse
Partridge
Pheasant
Woodcock
Chukar
Widgeon, Wood Duck

3-6 days aging time:
Turkey
Geese
Mallard, Pintail, Gadwall, Black Duck, Shoveler

Note: How you choose to age diving and sea ducks is based on personal preference and how strong of a fishy odor they carry. Some people prefer aging them, others refuse to age them. Experiment on your own to see what fits your personal taste.

Appendix D: Preparing Game Birds

Once birds have been cleaned, plucked or skinned and maybe aged a bit, they are ready to cook. The next step is preparing them for the recipe or cooking method. Whole birds are easy as they can be roasted, bagged, grilled or smoked. Cooking birds whole however, may not always be the best approach.

With game birds, their lack of fat predisposes them to drying out quickly. If birds have been skinned, something needs to be added to help replace that protection (bacon, spice paste, crust, etc.). Also keep in mind that breast meat cooks faster than leg and thigh meat and may be ruined with the whole-bird cooking method. One remedy is to fillet the breast meat off and continue cooking the leg and thigh meat, but this may impact your presentation. Moist-heat cooking methods help greatly when cooking whole birds. Smoking these birds is also beneficial as the meat cooks in the smoker but can be removed from the bones and added or cooked into another recipe that will then rehydrate it.

Another way to prepare birds, bone-in, is to cook the breast meat separate from the thigh and leg meat. Once separated, they tend to take about the same amount of cooking time.

A versatile and quick way to prepare game birds for cooking is to skin and cut the meat in cubes, slices or small chunks. Meat prepared in this way can be stir-fried, stewed, sauteed, poached or fried.

Grinding or dicing game bird meat makes for even more versatility as it can be made into nuggets or meatballs; mixed with ground pork, beef or chicken; or simply treated like any ground filling for tacos, spaghetti, gravy, casseroles or sandwich spreads.

Deboning game birds takes the guesswork out of cooking. Without bones, meat cooks evenly and can be stuffed with a variety of flavors and moisture-rich fats. Because game birds, by nature of the harvest, can carry a shot pellet or two in their flesh, the more they are handled, cut up and inspected, the less likely someone will need to visit the dentist after their meal.

PORTION SIZES FOR UPLAND BIRDS

1/2 turkey breast = 2 pheasants = 4 chukar/grouse = 6 pigeons = 8 quail = 10 doves

PORTION SIZES FOR WATERFOWL

1 greater Canada goose = 2 snow geese = 4 mallards = 8 wood ducks = 12 teal

Appreciate the differences in flavors of game birds. Each species is characteristically unique with its own flavor and texture. Never compare a wild bird with a domestically raised bird, for they can be as different as pork and beef.

BUTCHERING GAME BIRDS

Prior to cooking any game birds, breaking them down into body parts can separate some of the finer eating breast or thigh meat from the more sinuous legs and boney parts used in stock. Remember, it is the law to retrieve all edible body parts of upland birds and waterfowl. People who cut out the breast and toss the rest of the carcass are in violation of the law because they are discarding edible leg and thigh meat.

There are a couple options when it comes to breaking down birds prior to cooking them, and the more time you spend doing it, the more you'll discover what suits your personal needs. Typically, birds are broken down once they've been skinned, as it's challenging to keep the skin in-tact when cutting wild birds into parts.

One skinned, take the carcass and lay it on its back. Push down on the legs, forcing them away from the body, until the ball-and-socket joint separate. With a sharp knife, cut though the muscles at the hip joint, keeping as much of the upper thigh and lower back muscles as possible.

On larger fowl like turkeys, swans, cranes and geese, the thigh meet can be separated from the drumstick. If cleaning a lot of birds, separating the tasty thigh from the tougher, more sinuous drumstick allows you to cook them independently of one another.

The entire breast bone and keel can be separated from the spine, ribs and neck, with both sides of the breast meat intact. To do this, simply pull the ribs away from the breast, separating the ribs. Next, cut the breast away from the wings, at the shoulder joint.

Once this process is complete, you're left with a whole breast (the meat still attached to both sides), a pair of legs and thighs, and a backbone with ribs and neck attached. The spine, neck and ribs make for excellent stock.

If looking to breast-out your birds, that's simple and quick, and should be done prior to breaking down the carcass. Start by cutting away the skin from both sides of the breast, all the way down to the base of the wings and the back of the rib cage. Next, take a sharp fillet knife and slice into the breast, keeping the blade firmly running against the keel as you cut. Continue filleting the meat away from the keel and breast bone until removed from the bone. Sever the chunk of breast meat where it attaches to the shoulder, at the base of the wing, and repeat on the other side.

This leaves you with two complete pieces of breast meat. From there, simply continue removing the skin of the bird, piecing the legs, thighs and other parts as you go, as described above.

GRINDING GAME BIRDS

As with wild game meat, we never mix any kind of fat into the grinding process of our birds. If adding another meat is desired, we do that right before cooking, not before freezing the meat. When cooking ground game birds, use plenty of olive oil in the pan to prevent the meat from sticking and drying out. Do not overcook delicate ground meat.

Many game birds have a soft textured meat. A fine chop/dice may be all that is needed for the meat to resemble ground meat. A few pulses in a food processor or mini-chopper can also accomplish "grinding" the meat.

DEBONING GAME BIRDS

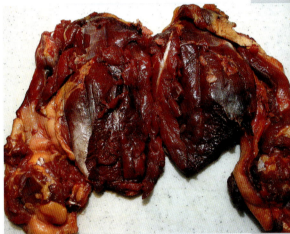

Deboning an entire game bird sounds more intimidating that it really is. In fact, the deboning process is easy, it just takes time.

Deboning a bird is just like deboning a fish or big game animal. As long as you keep reminding yourself that the objective of deboning is to removing the muscles from the bone, you'll be fine.

Place the skinned carcass on it's breast, backbone facing you and parallel to the counter. With a sharp knife begin carving your way down one side of the bird, separating the meat from the muscle (fillet one side of the bird at a time). Work all the way from the neck, down to the thigh meat. The purpose is to cut and peel the meat away from the bone, working around the side of the bird and eventually to the front.

When cutting around the wing area, make as few slices as possible to get the muscles away from the boney structures. When cutting around the legs of small birds, some of the muscles can be left intact and pulled over the leg bones; on bigger birds a section of leg muscle may need to be cut so you can free the rest of the sinuous muscles from the bone.

Once you've filleted the back, wing and leg muscles, continue to the breast. Be sure to keep the knife blade riding against the breast bone in order to retain as much meat as possible. Continue filleting up the breast bone and keel, stopping when you reach the cartilaginous ridge. From there, flip the bird back on its breast and repeat the filleting process for the other side.

As you cut through the second breast, be careful not to separate the meat as you work toward the breast bone and keel. Keep the cuts close to the bone, ensuring both filleted halves remain intact. The final cut is made down the ridge of the breast bone, ensuring that all the meat remains connected in one piece.

The deboning process does take a while, so be patient. The more of these you do, the faster you'll get at it, and the more cooking opportunities you'll have at your fingertips.

Wondering what to do with a deboned bird? See page 43 for Turkpheasquail or page 106 for Boneless Duck Roast. Try combining game birds you have available. A 3-bird roast may be a small goose with a chukar and a teal, "Goochukduck?" If feeling daring, and you have the resources, try a 5-bird roast consisting of turkey, goose, chicken, pheasant and pigeon. Any of these combinations can be enhanced by spicy meat and bread stuffings such as sausage and cornbread.

The cooking options don't stop with the meat you've just removed. The entire skeleton can now be used to make a tasty stock. With this method, absolutely nothing goes to waste.

MARINADES & BRINES

Marinades and brines help flavor, tenderize and protect game birds during the cooking process. Flavors are endless and can be combined in many ways to please all tastes. Acids in these liquids help to break-down the proteins in meats making them more tender as well as enhancing the flavor. Oil added to marinades—especially wild game—helps prevent moisture loss in cooking and also protects meat if cooking with dry-cooking methods such as grilling.

Acids include vinegars, citrus, wine, spirits, tomato, fruit juices and yogurt.

Flavors include herbs, spices, garlic, ginger, honey, soy sauce and hot sauce, to name a few. Any oil will work in a marinade but stronger flavored oils such as sesame or walnut oil will help add flavor as well.

Depending on meat type, marinade time usually varies from 30 minutes to overnight. Many marinades double as basting liquids.

SOAKING SOLUTIONS

Most game birds will benefit from a quick soak in a lightly salted water solution to draw blood from the meat. The following suggestions work with stronger flavored ducks and geese and also help tenderize older turkeys.

- Buttermilk
- Strong brewed coffee (cooled)
- Tomato juice or Bloody Mary mix
- 1 cup apple juice + 1 cup beef broth (waterfowl) or chicken broth (upland birds)
- 2 cups milk + 2 tablespoons vinegar or lemon juice
- 2 cups water + 1/2 teaspoon salt + 1/2 teaspoon baking soda
- 1 cup water + 1/2 cup vinegar + onion stuffed in body cavity

Other "taming" flavors include oranges, ginger, sauerkraut, onions, celery, BBQ sauce and curries. See section, *Sauces, Rubs, Marinades & More,* for additional suggestions.

THERMOMETERS

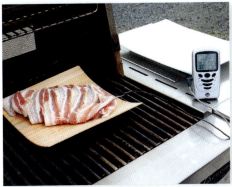

When cooking wild game and fish, use an internal cooking thermometer. With these lean, delicate meats, just a degree or two of overcooking can drastically impact the end result of a dish. Probe-style thermometers work better on smaller, thinner cuts of wild game birds.

INTERNAL TEMPERATURE

Recommended internal cooking temperatures for game birds vary greatly, from USDA recommendations of all birds cooking to 165° to waterfowl connoisseurs who never let their ducks go beyond 130°. There is quite a bit of personal preference involved here, but if the meat has been handled properly, there is little worry of any bacteria that may cause a food-born illness when cooked to 140°. We usually aim for 140° and then taste for tenderness. Some birds taste better cooked to "falling-off-the-bone" while others get stronger flavored and become tougher. Find out what methods work best with the birds you harvest. Take notes, experiment and perfect your skills through trial and error.

TEMPERATURE RECOMMENDATIONS

Turkey Whole: 150°-160°
Turkey Ground or Stuffed: 165°
Upland Game Birds: 150°-160°
Waterfowl: 130° = rare, 140° = medium rare, 150° = medium, 160° = well done

PRECOOKING METHODS

Although they can stand alone, these methods are well suited when a recipe calls for "cooked game meat." Cooked game meat can also simply mean "leftovers"–meat that is left over from roasting or cooking birds whole.

POACHING

Poach boneless game meat in water or turkey/chicken stock or broth. In a saucepan, bring to a boil, reduce to medium heat, cover and cook 15+ minutes (the larger the pieces, the longer the poaching time).

Poach whole birds the same way, extending cooking time to 30-40 minutes. Birds can be poached in the oven, in a casserole dish, in a single layer. Cover with boiling liquid. Bake in a preheated 400° oven 25-35 minutes or until internal temperature reaches 160°.

STEAMING

Steam according to manufacturers instructions on steamer. Steam approximately as long as suggested for poultry or to 160°.

SMOKING

See Game Bird Jerky, page 110 or Smoked Turkey, page 45 or Smoked Pheasant, page 80.

CROCK POT

If cooking birds for another recipe, simply put birds in crock pot with a few cups of turkey/chicken stock or broth, season if desired and cook on high 4-5 hours or on low 7-8 hours.

PRESSURE COOKER

For best flavor, sear meat in 1 tablespoon olive oil, add 1-2 cups turkey/chicken stock or broth, season if desired. Bring liquid in pressure cooker to a boil, put lid on and cook under high pressure. Follow manufacturers directions for times or general rule for high-pressure: Boneless or pieces of birds 8-10 minutes; 2-3 pound birds 15-20 minutes; 3-4 pound birds 20-25 minutes. Let pressure release on its own.

MOIST HEAT METHODS

Braising	Clay Pot
Steaming	Dutch Oven
Poaching	Oven Bag
Crock Pot	Parchment Paper

DRY HEAT METHODS

Sauteing	Deep Frying
Pan Frying	Roasting
Grilling	Broiling

Stuffing Note: When cooking a stuffed bird, realize that the stuffing slows down the cooking time and may dry out the meat. Take special care to add fat or some kind of protective covering over the meat so it doesn't dry out (bacon, vegetables, crust, etc), basting frequently. Stuffed birds can also be cooked in a bag.

PLANK COOKING
(See Appendix F, page 148)

PROTECTIVE METHODS

These methods help keep both plucked and skinned game birds moist. Thought of like a "second skin," add bacon or a sheet of pork fat (barding), sausage or the skin of a chicken as a coating with any dry-heat cooking method. Slurries, pastes and wet rubs also help protect game birds while cooking. Salt, flour or pie crusts sealed around whole birds or bird breasts not only make a dazzling presentation, they keep moisture in the bird so even though a dry-heat method is used for cooking, the bird is also steaming inside the crust.

Appendix E: Preserving Game Birds

Limited out, now what? Getting birds can be the easy part–preparing them is the work and eating them is the reward. The goal in our house is to eat as much as we can when it comes home fresh and in-season. With game birds, that isn't always possible. There can be large bag limits, consecutive hunting days and multi-party hunts. All of this can add up to a lot of meat that must be preserved.

Whether freezing, canning, smoking or making stock, all of these methods add up to easy and quick meals later in the year. Many game birds require special care and do not stand up to freezing for long periods of time. We never worry about our venison losing its quality after several months in the deep freeze but we take special care not to let our game birds freeze too long.

FREEZING BIRDS & SMOKING USE

Birds can be frozen with feathers on (gutted), as this is a great way to prevent freezer burn. This approach takes up more freezer space and makes for more work prior to cooking time. Many people like to freeze plucked birds in large cubes of ice (again, a great method but takes extra space). We prefer vacuum sealing and freezing birds (be sure there are no sharp bones which can puncture the bag). Prior to freezing, always wash and dry birds after gutting and plucking.

We don't recommend freezing ducks that have fed off sea life as their strong flavors tend to concentrate during the freezing process. Use these ducks

example, we rely on Oregon State Home Extension as our official resource on home canning.

STOCK

There isn't a bird carcass in our house that doesn't usually make it into the stock pot for a render. Simply grab whatever vegetables and herbs are on-hand, add them to the pot with the carcass, salt and pepper to taste, fill the pot with water and simmer for 6-8 hours. If desiring condensed stock, let the water boil down. If wanting ready-to-use stock, add water a few times while it is simmering. The only birds we don't use for stock are sea ducks, fish eating ducks and any strong "gamey" birds.

Some of the best stock is made from birds that have been smoked, whole. After cleaning the meat off the bones, fill up the stock pot and follow the above steps for stock. Do not salt the stock until it has simmered a few hours as it will be salty due to the smoking process.

Stock can also be made with raw game birds. Basically poached, the meat can be removed from the bones when it is done (internal thermometer reading of 160°) and the carcass returned to the pot where it can continue simmering.

To freeze stock, cool in the refrigerator then strain and discard all bones, vegetables, herbs and/or spices. Ladle into clean glass jars, plastic freezer containers or sealable plastic bags. Label and freeze. If specific spices or flavors have been added, note that on the label (i.e. Asian Stock may have ginger and lemongrass in it and Italian Stock may have rosemary and thyme).

Many of the recipes in this book call for turkey/chicken stock or broth. Use the broth you have in the freezer for an economical and healthier alternative to store-bought stocks and broths.

in fresh recipes or make jerky for best results.

Smaller birds should be used up within three months of freezing. Larger birds and turkey can go six months. When we see birds stack-up in the freezer, getting close to the cut-off recommendation, we will pull them all out and fire-up the smoker. Smoked meat can be used right away or vacuum sealed and refrozen to use in another recipe.

CANNING BIRDS

Having home-canned turkey or other game birds can be a great, fast-food option. Since birds are fully cooked in the canning process they only need to be seasoned and reheated for an easy meal. Always follow specific recipes from a reliable canning source. For

Appendix F:
Plank Cooking & Wood Wraps

The process of cooking food on cut wood dates back to Native American cultures on both the East and West coasts of North America. Plank cooking and cooking on wood wraps are cooking styles that promote enhanced smokey flavors and help keep moisture in lean foods.

Game birds are very lean and tend to dry out when dry cooking methods like grilling are used to prepare them. Add a plank or a wrap when grilling and oven baking to protect and flavor game birds. Plank cooking helps retain the moisture by providing a barrier between the meat and heat source while simultaneously imparting steam from the soaked board, into foods. The smokey flavors derived from plank cooking pair well with game birds and enhance virtually any recipe.

Planks can be purchased "ready-to-use" or *untreated* wood can be bought at a lumber yard and planks can be cut to desired size. Any non-resinous wood can be plank cooked upon; cedar, alder, oak, maple, cherry, apple, pecan and hickory are a some of the more common wood types. If cutting your own planks from trees, be sure to dry or season them as you would for firewood.

Planks and wood wraps are becoming more popular and easier to find. Check the meat department of local grocery stores, kitchen stores or the internet for wrap availability.

Planks and wraps not only affect the flavor and texture of the food presented, they make clean-up easy. Planks and wraps keep grill grates clean of any food residue, are natural deodorizers when cooking smells (like fish) are overpowering in the kitchen or travel trailer, and they also make a novel serving presentation. When else can you burn the serving platter instead of washing it?

Some planks can be used several times. When oven planking, planks can be used indefinitely–a simple sanding with abrasive paper will refresh them to their original state in no time. When using direct grilling heat, planks may only be used one time. When indirect grilling, where planks are not repeatedly catching fire, they can be washed and reused several times. Wraps can only be used one time.

PLANK PREPARATION

STEP 1: Soak plank in water or suggested liquid, minimum 1 hour, maximum 24 hours.

STEP 2: Preheat plank on grill at medium heat 2-3 minutes, or in a 350° oven 5 minutes.

STEP 3: Brush a light coating of olive oil onto cooking side of board if desired to prevent food sticking.

PLANK COOKING OPTIONS:

GRILL (DIRECT HEAT): Use the lowest setting on a gas grill or low charcoal heat. Place plank with food directly over the heat source. Cook with the lid closed so smoke surrounds food and infuses flavor. Plank should reach heavy smoke in 15-20 minutes. When plank begins to smoke, check often–use spray bottle filled with water to extinguish any flame on the plank. This apporach promotes a heavy smoke flavor.

GRILL (INDIRECT HEAT): Use a medium setting on a gas grill. If using charcoal, pile coals to one side. Place plank opposite the heat source. Cook with lid closed so smoke surrounds food and infuses flavor. Plank should begin to smoke after 15-20 minutes. The plank should not catch fire using this method. Cooking time increases due to the lower temperature. This method promotes a light smoke flavor.

OVEN: Preheat oven and board to 350° or as stated in recipe. Place plank with food, directly on oven rack. Position a foil lined baking sheet on the rack below the plank to catch any drippings. This method infuses a light smoke essence into food. Planks can be reused.

WORDS OF CAUTION
- Never leave planks unattended on the grill or campfire.
- Avoid repeatedly opening the grill cover as this can cause flare-ups and lost heat.
- Do not stand directly over the grill when opening, as there can be a lot of smoke.
- Be careful not to inhale smoke or allow it to billow into the eyes.
- Monitor fatty foods for more flare-ups as fat drips off the plank.
- When using a plank in the oven, use a baking sheet to catch any drips.

If serving food directly off a plank or wrap, or moving either with the food still on it, be certain to place it on a safe surface. The underside of the wood is extremely hot and can cause some surfaces to melt or catch fire. Having a large metal spatula with which to lift and transport the wood is a good idea and allows for easy placement on to a large plate. Do not to bring a burning or smoldering plank inside the house.

WRAP PREPARATION

STEP 1: Soak wrap in water or suggested liquid 10-15 minutes.
STEP 2: Place food on moist wrap, roll closed and secure with a metal clip or kitchen twine.
STEP 3: Always cook on indirect heat on a grill and do not cook in an oven exceeding 350°.

Index

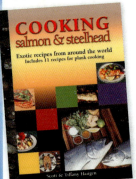
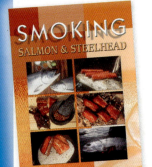